THE AMERICAN PRESIDENTS SERIES

Joyce Appleby on *Thomas Jefferson*
Louis Auchincloss on *Theodore Roosevelt*
H. W. Brands on *Woodrow Wilson*
Douglas Brinkley on *Gerald Ford*
James MacGregor Burns and Susan Dunn on *George Washington*
Robert Dallek on *James Monroe*
John W. Dean on *Warren Harding*
John Patrick Diggins on *John Adams*
E. L. Doctorow on *Abraham Lincoln*
Henry F. Graff on *Grover Cleveland*
Roy Jenkins on *Franklin Delano Roosevelt*
Zachary Karabell on *Chester A. Arthur*
William E. Leuchtenburg on *Herbert Hoover*
Kevin Phillips on *William McKinley*
Robert V. Remini on *John Quincy Adams*
John Seigenthaler on *James K. Polk*
Hans L. Trefousse on *Rutherford B. Hayes*
Tom Wicker on *Dwight D. Eisenhower*
Ted Widmer on *Martin Van Buren*
Sean Wilentz on *Andrew Jackson*
Garry Wills on *James Madison*

The Emerging Republican Majority

*Mediacracy: American Parties and
Politics in the Communications Age*

Post-Conservative America

*Staying on Top: The Business Case for a
National Industrial Strategy*

The Politics of Rich and Poor

*Boiling Point: Democrats, Republicans
and the Decline of Middle-Class Prosperity*

*Arrogant Capitol: Washington, Wall Street
and the Frustration of American Politics*

*The Cousins' Wars: Religion, Politics and the
Triumph of Anglo-America*

*Wealth and Democracy: A Political
History of the American Rich*

William
McKinley

Kevin Phillips

William
McKinley

THE AMERICAN PRESIDENTS

ARTHUR M. SCHLESINGER, JR., GENERAL EDITOR

Times Books

HENRY HOLT AND COMPANY, NEW YORK

Times Books
Henry Holt and Company, LLC
Publishers since 1866
115 West 18th Street
New York, New York 10011

Henry Holt® is a registered trademark of Henry Holt and Company, LLC.

LIBRARY OF CONGRESS CATALOGING-IN-PUBLICATION DATA
Phillips, Kevin.
William McKinley / Kevin Phillips.—1st ed.
p. cm.—(The American presidents)
Includes bibliographical references (p.) and index.
ISBN 0-8050-6953-4
1. McKinley, William, 1843–1901. 2. Presidents—United States—Biography.
3. United States—Politics and government—1897–1901. I. Title. II. American
presidents series
(Times Books (Firm))
E711.6.P47 2003
973.8'8'092—dc21
[B]   2003050701

Henry Holt books are available for special promotions and premiums.
For details contact: Director, Special Markets.

First Edition 2003

Printed in the United States of America
1   3   5   7   9   10   8   6   4   2

TO

WALTER DEAN BURNHAM

AND

SAMUEL LUBELL

who introduced me to the meaning
of the election of 1896

Contents

Editor's Note

THE AMERICAN PRESIDENCY

The president is the central player in the American political order. That would seem to contradict the intentions of the Founding Fathers. Remembering the horrid example of the British monarchy, they invented a separation of powers in order, as Justice Brandeis later put it, "to preclude the exercise of arbitrary power." Accordingly, they divided the government into three allegedly equal and coordinate branches—the executive, the legislative, and the judiciary.

But a system based on the tripartite separation of powers has an inherent tendency toward inertia and stalemate. One of the three branches must take the initiative if the system is to move. The executive branch alone is structurally capable of taking that initiative. The Founders must have sensed this when they accepted Alexander Hamilton's proposition in the Seventieth Federalist that "energy in the executive is a leading character in the definition of good government." They thus envisaged a strong president—but within an equally strong system of constitutional accountability. (The term *imperial presidency* arose in the 1970s to describe the situation when the balance between power and accountability is upset in favor of the executive.)

The American system of self-government thus comes to focus in the presidency—"the vital place of action in the system," as Woodrow Wilson put it. Henry Adams, himself the great-grandson and grandson of presidents as well as the most brilliant of American historians, said that the American president "resembles the commander of a ship at sea. He must have a helm to grasp, a course to steer, a port to seek." The men in the White House (thus far only men, alas) in steering their chosen courses have shaped our destiny as a nation.

Biography offers an easy education in American history, rendering the past more human, more vivid, more intimate, more accessible, more connected to ourselves. Biography reminds us that presidents are not supermen. They are human beings too, worrying about decisions, attending to wives and children, juggling balls in the air, and putting on their pants one leg at a time. Indeed, as Emerson contended, "There is properly no history; only biography."

Presidents serve us as inspirations, and they also serve us as warnings. They provide bad examples as well as good. The nation, the Supreme Court has said, has "no right to expect that it will always have wise and humane rulers, sincerely attached to the principles of the Constitution. Wicked men, ambitious of power, with hatred of liberty and contempt of law, may fill the place once occupied by Washington and Lincoln."

The men in the White House express the ideal and the values, the frailties and the flaws, of the voters who send them there. It is altogether natural that we should want to know more about the virtues and the vices of the fellows we have elected to govern us. As we know more about them, we will know more about ourselves. The French political philosopher Joseph de Maistre said, "Every nation has the government it deserves."

At the start of the twenty-first century, forty-two men have made it to the Oval Office. (George W. Bush is counted our forty-third president, because Grover Cleveland, who served nonconsecutive terms, is counted twice.) Of the parade of presidents, a dozen or so lead the polls periodically conducted by historians and political scientists. What makes a great president?

Great presidents possess, or are possessed by, a vision of an ideal America. Their passion, as they grasp the helm, is to set the ship of state on the right course toward the port they seek. Great presidents also have a deep psychic connection with the needs, anxieties, dreams of people. "I do not believe," said Wilson, "that any man can lead who does not act . . . under the impulse of a profound sympathy with those whom he leads—a sympathy which is insight—an insight which is of the heart rather than of the intellect."

"All of our great presidents," said Franklin D. Roosevelt, "were leaders of thought at a time when certain ideas in the life of the nation had to be clarified." So Washington incarnated the idea of federal union, Jefferson and Jackson the idea of democracy, Lincoln union and freedom, Cleveland rugged honesty. Theodore Roosevelt and Wilson, said FDR, were both "moral leaders, each in his own way and his own time, who used the presidency as a pulpit."

To succeed, presidents must not only have a port to seek but they must convince Congress and the electorate that it is a port worth seeking. Politics in a democracy is ultimately an educational process, an adventure in persuasion and consent. Every president stands in Theodore Roosevelt's bully pulpit.

The greatest presidents in the scholars' rankings, Washington, Lincoln, and Franklin Roosevelt, were leaders who confronted and overcame the republic's greatest crises. Crisis widens presidential opportunities for bold and imaginative action. But it does not guarantee presidential greatness. The crisis of secession did not spur Buchanan or the crisis of depression spur Hoover to creative leadership. Their inadequacies in the face of crisis allowed Lincoln and the second Roosevelt to show the difference individuals make to history. Still, even in the absence of first-order crisis, forceful and persuasive presidents—Jefferson, Jackson, Theodore Roosevelt, Ronald Reagan—are able to impose their own priorities on the country.

The diverse drama of the presidency offers a fascinating set of tales. Biographies of American presidents constitute a chronicle of wisdom and folly, nobility and pettiness, courage and cunning, forthrightness and deceit, quarrel and consensus. The turmoil perennially swirling around the White House illuminates the heart of the American democracy.

It is the aim of the American Presidents series to present the grand panorama of our chief executives in volumes compact enough for the busy reader, lucid enough for the student, authoritative enough for the scholar. Each volume offers a distillation of character and career. I hope that these lives will give readers some understanding of the pitfalls and potentialities of the presidency and also of the responsibilities of citizenship. Truman's famous sign—"The buck stops here"—tells only half the story. Citizens cannot escape the ultimate responsibility. It is in the voting booth, not on the presidential desk, that the buck finally stops.

—Arthur M. Schlesinger, Jr.

Introduction

Even the work of talented biographers and historians has not shaken the picture of this president as a hidebound Republican conservative whose ideas were obsolete before his death and whose career was only a prelude to the excitement of the Theodore Roosevelt years.
Lewis Gould, *The Presidency of William McKinley*

By any serious measurement, William McKinley was a major American president. His life is all the more interesting for achieving so much, stealthily but honorably, behind the "masks that he wore," in the words of Julia Foraker, the wife of one of his home-state rivals, U.S. Senator Joseph B. Foraker.

He more than met the usual criteria. McKinley was among the sixteen U.S. presidents (of forty-three) elected to or serving two terms. He was among the thirteen of these who, unlike Grant, Nixon, and Clinton, avoided major scandal or impeachment. Of the post–Civil War dynasty of seven Ohio-born presidents from Grant to Harding, his preeminence is obvious.

McKinley's was the administration during which the United States made its diplomatic and military debut as a world power. He was one of the eight presidents who, either in the White House or on the battlefield, stood as principals in successful wars, and he was among the six or seven to take office in what became recognized as a major realignment of the U.S. party system. No other Republican nominee could have made of the 1896 election what McKinley did—and no other Republican would have had the stature and self-assuredness to take Theodore Roosevelt as his ticket mate in 1900.

Superficially, meeting all these criteria puts the Ohioan in the rare company of Washington, Jackson, Lincoln, and Franklin D.

Roosevelt. Yet hardly anyone thinks of him that way. The recent consensus of historians has pegged him somewhere in the ho-hum midsection of presidential ratings, and small wonder. Too many dismissive paragraphs, thoughtless sentences, and inaccurate descriptions still nurture the false public impression of a cultural and intellectual mediocrity, however popular, who toadied to business as a puppet of Wall Street. Biographers like Lewis Gould, H. Wayne Thompson, and Margaret Leech have had the matter largely right: that too many of their colleagues have indeed had it largely wrong.

There was a time, back in trolley car days, when McKinley was much better regarded: certainly into the 1920s and in some chronicles later. More than fifty years ago, I saved my pennies as a boy to buy mint U.S. postage stamps of the "Presidential Series of 1937" then in everyday use. A child's history lesson in itself, this set began with the green one-cent Washington, the red two-cent Adams, and the purple three-cent Jefferson, ascending through the ten-cent Tyler and sixteen-cent Lincoln to the twenty-five-cent McKinley, perfectly matching the order in which the chief executives had served. There was no twenty-four-cent stamp, because Grover Cleveland, whose two terms were separated by four years of Benjamin Harrison, was both the twenty-second and the twenty-fourth president.

Number twenty-five, McKinley, was notable in my ten-year-old eyes for marking the end of historical exactitude and transition to modernity. The presidents of the new century who had already died were not treated as history. Number twenty-six, Theodore Roosevelt, was assigned to the thirty-cent stamp; William Howard Taft, number twenty-seven, had his jowly visage imprinted on the fifty-cent stamp, and so on through Woodrow Wilson (a dollar), Warren Harding (two dollars), and Calvin Coolidge (five dollars). I never bought the Harding or Coolidge stamps because both were accounted lightweights; besides, the Harding stamp cost eight Saturday movies and Coolidge's twenty. From this series, McKinley became a bridge president to me—a transition executive between another century's remoteness and the current one's immediacy. The old 1925-ish histories one could buy along New York City's "Book Row" in 1951 for ten or twenty-five cents spoke well of him, but not at much length. The greater decline in McKinley's stature came as the 1932–1968 New Deal Democratic era and its dismissal of business, tariffs, and gold standards swept the day.

During the fifties, my interest in our nation's chief executives shifted from portraits on postage stamps into a new and more serious channel: charting and mapping the county-level, district-level, and state-level voting patterns of U.S. presidential elections. The crumbling, browned pages of old election data available in the run of dime-each World Almanacs did not go back past 1916, but McKinley soon became well known to me because of his victory in 1896. He was the political architect who ended the two-decade national stalemate existing since 1876, turning a weakened Civil War coalition to a new full-fledged industrial GOP majority (1896–1932). That made him the most important nineteenth-century Republican after Lincoln.

By 1960, my maps and charts had convinced me that another realignment was in sight to end the old Civil War division of U.S. politics, displace the New Deal alignment, and give the GOP a new variety of presidential-level majority. The result was my first book, *The Emerging Republican Majority*, used in the 1968 Republican campaign and published in 1969.

McKinley reclaimed my serious attention in the 1990s when my book writing turned back to history. *The Cousins' Wars* (1999) examined the three great English-speaking civil wars—the English Civil War, the American Revolution, and the American Civil War—as prime molding forces of the relationship between the United States and Britain. After the tensions of the years 1861 to 1865, those ties finally returned to entente, never again broken, in the new global power context that arose out of McKinley's Spanish-American War. My next book, *Wealth and Democracy* (2002), developed as one of its subthemes how the GOP began each of its cycles in power (1860, 1896, and 1968) with a broad-based economics and sympathy to labor. Proof could be found in the Lincoln-Johnson-Grant era, under McKinley and Theodore Roosevelt, and then again under Richard Nixon and his hoped-for New American Majority. The market-manic, speculative, survival-of-the-fittest mentality came late in the cycle. McKinley's views, I discovered, put him in the realignment, not plutocratic, mode. Absent this insufficiently recognized appeal, he wouldn't have become president in 1896.

The upshot was a gnawing curiosity about McKinley's personality, presidency, and hidden abilities. Who really was he? What did he achieve? Why didn't I have a fuller picture—and what forces had led to him being so widely and unfairly dismissed?

It has not been for want of good biographies, as the bibliography at this book's end will attest. But in some places even these have muted their revisionism or indulged one or more of the caricatures that dog McKinley's reputation.

This is an introduction, and, as such, a premature locus for tackling dismissive stereotypes. However, the notion of a picture being worth a thousand words fits the lasting damage of cartoons run by the "Yellow Press" in 1896 and 1900, amplified after the 1920s by the ideological slights of progressive and New Deal commentators. These calumnies have continued to outweigh what, collectively, has been six or eight hundred thousand words of better, fairer biographical evidence. Here I will simply introduce the six unjust dismissals:

- The image spread in the election of 1896, notably by the Hearst cartoonist Homer Davenport, of McKinley as a puppet of plutocratic "boss" Mark Hanna.
- The portraiture of McKinley as a culture-free, unlettered, tasteless Middle West precursor of Sinclair Lewis's George Babbitt—suitable attributes for a political hack.
- The false vignettes of the Spanish-American War—a McKinley with "the backbone of a chocolate eclair" (in TR's words), but also a president who drew the United States willy-nilly into imperialism and an East Asian commitment that ultimately led to disaster in Vietnam.
- The supposedly reactionary role of McKinley in shaping the late-nineteenth-century U.S. protective tariff, dismissed by twentieth-century Anglo-American economic fashion.
- The burden, hardly of the dead president's own making, that his assassination in 1901 denied him the last forty-two months of a reform-trending second term and left Progressivism to be associated with the sparkle of Theodore Roosevelt.

• The tendency of post-1933 opinion molders to dismiss the two-term Republican presidents of bourgeois taste and conservative politics—Eisenhower and Reagan, as well as McKinley—as of no more than middle rank despite considerable accomplishments in challenging periods.

McKinley was no Washington or Lincoln. This portrait will describe an upright and effective president of the solid second rank. His insistence on making friends, orchestrating consensus, and avoiding acrimony probably bars him from the first rank. As for his problems of being overshadowed by TR, shouldn't assassinations in fairness require some explanations of what would or might have been? This book will make a case, in chapter 5, that the McKinley and Roosevelt administrations make greatest sense as a continuum.

The tendency of twentieth-century opinion molders to underrate effective two-term Republican presidents of middle-brow mien is one strand in my concluding chapter. Rebuilding the middle-class fabric of a torn and divided nation is an achievement for which GOP presidents, not least William McKinley, have gotten too little credit.

In sum, the evidence supports a hitherto minority viewpoint: that great political skill, national commitment, and personal strength—used on behalf of much more reformism than is usually recognized—lurked behind McKinley's inscrutability, his tactical avoidance of written or public policy commitment, and his oratorical preference for the blandiloquent. Just by itself, his draining preoccupation with an invalid wife was something friends thought almost qualified him for sainthood. John Hay, who was Abraham Lincoln's private secretary, Alexander Hamilton's acclaimed biographer, a collector of Renaissance paintings, and McKinley's ambassador to Britain and secretary of state, summed up in 1896 that "We who know him regard him as a man of extraordinary ability, integrity and force of character."

Henry Kissinger was not, of course, the first secretary of state to flatter a president. However, the collective tributes of men like Hay, TR, Elihu Root, Charles G. Dawes, Philander Knox, Leonard Wood, George Cortelyou, and William Howard Taft. McKinley's staff and cabinet appointments, like Lincoln's, launched the next Republican generation—support a reassessment. If we cannot put William McKinley in the small circle of great chief executives, he certainly deserves admission to the six- or eight-president second tier.

As I write, further attention is being drawn to McKinley's achievements by Karl Rove, the political adviser to President Bush. The idea that McKinley's 1896 to 1900 realignment might be a model for the Republicans from 2000 to 2004 has some plausibility. McKinley, after all, managed to take an earlier GOP majority framework that reached back thirty-odd years and give it new life and a somewhat different and updated coalition. Where the parallel weakens is that McKinley was a much more progressive Republican. Readers will see that in Ohio and Washington, he embraced labor, favored spreading more of the tax burden onto the rich, not less, and, from his years in Congress, was so contemptuous of lobbyists and their practices that in 1897, he rejected one of Mark Hanna's proposed appointments by saying he would not have a lobbyist in his cabinet. In 1898, McKinley also held back rather than promote the rush to war with Spain. These and dozens of other little-noticed viewpoints further amplify why our twenty-fifth president deserves much better of history and historians.

Part I

Ohio Born and Molded

1

William McKinley, Ohioan

It is generally believed by strangers that the most interesting and significant part of Ohio's history lies in the part the state has played in
national politics—as a "barometer" state and as the home of political
leaders. Ohio has produced many men of political importance, and has
sent seven native sons to the presidency—Grant, Garfield, Hayes, Benjamin Harrison, McKinley, Taft and Harding. However, Ohio's industrial life overshadows its politics. . . . Ohio's major importance—and
major interest—lies in a large and varied industrialism.

The Ohio Guide (WPA)

William McKinley was born in Ohio in 1843, mostly educated
there, fought the Civil War in a Buckeye regiment, represented an
Ohio district in Congress, and sat in the governor's chair in Columbus. He loved the state. His God, loved even more, was the benign
God of an Ohio Methodist Sunday School. His career is only
understandable as the career of a proud and well-connected middle-
class Ohioan. Factory whistles were his Mozart wind concertos, tariff schedules his Plato's *Republic,* and Civil War recollections his
Herodotus.

Nineteenth-century Ohio, however, was not just a place but a
phenomenon. No retrospective on America's twenty-fifth president
can begin without a comprehension of the state's spectacular emergence as a center of U.S. political and economic gravity during the
fifty-eight years between McKinley's birth and death. Like Virginia
earlier, Ohio became a "Mother of Presidents." It was also the first
crucible of the Old Northwest. In the year McKinley was born, four
other future GOP presidents called Ohio home—Ulysses Grant,
just out of West Point, Rutherford Hayes, a year past his Kenyon

College graduation, the twelve-year-old James Garfield, working to support his widowed mother, and Benjamin Harrison, a schoolboy in North Bend.

None, obviously, had any youthful inkling of the Ohio regime to come, of how from 1868 to 1900, no Republican would be elected president who was not born in the Buckeye State. Those of other origins tried in vain: New Yorkers, Hoosiers, state of Maine men, anyone. Even the three leading Northern generals in the Civil War were Ohio-born: Grant, William Tecumseh Sherman, and Philip Sheridan. Ohio itself was the sole Northern state central enough to be a bridge from the war's eastern theater of operations in next-door Virginia to its western theater spanning the Ohio-Mississippi river system. The late nineteenth century was Ohio's great period, the Buckeye hour in history.

This unique molding and mentoring helped to sculpt McKinley's political rise and influence. The state's economic vigor and innovation, besides underpinning its national importance, also gave McKinley his principal career theme: first, the blessings of a protective tariff system, and then the reforms it would need to meet the twentieth century. Lacking the patina that other Ohio GOP presidents got at Williams College (Garfield), Yale (Taft), or Harvard Law School (Hayes), little about McKinley did not reflect his middle-class, midcountry origins.

DRUMS TO DYNAMOS ALONG THE OHIO

At the beginning of the nineteenth century, Ohio was the doorstep of the New West, the open, rich land closest to Virginia and the original Northern states. Steamboats were common on the Ohio River by the 1820s. By 1830 and 1840, the center of national population was speeding westward across Virginia. In 1850 it hovered near Parkersburg, West Virginia, on the south bank of the Ohio River. Then, like Eliza, the fugitive slave in Harriet Beecher Stowe's *Uncle Tom's Cabin*, it leaped across the river, coming to rest in 1860 about fifteen miles from Chillicothe.

Ohio had gone from territory to state in 1803, just as Thomas Jefferson was arranging the Louisiana Purchase. The early settlers, disproportionately from Pennsylvania, Virginia, and Kentucky, concentrated near the river that had taken most of them west. Cincinnati, its "Queen City," became the state's major urban and commercial center, although its streets were often clogged by noisy, dirty hogs on their way to the slaughterhouses.

Then in the 1830s, courtesy of New York's Erie Canal, a new population movement began to fill up the northern and central parts of the state with Yankees, Pennsylvanians, New Yorkers, and German, British, and Irish immigrants. At midcentury, Cincinnati still had a huge edge over Yankee Cleveland on Lake Erie—a population of some 115,000 versus just 17,000. But growth in northern Ohio was accelerating like one of the new Philadelphia-built locomotives on the Mad River and Lake Erie Railway.

Ohio was a new type of state, a composition board of converging migrations from all three major U.S. eighteenth-century coastal regions—New England, the Middle Atlantic (mostly Pennsylvanians and New Yorkers), and the South (principally Virginians, Carolinians, and migrants from Tennessee and Kentucky). Ohio's northeast, the former Western Reserve of Connecticut, had welcomed a small first wave of Yankee settlers in the 1780s and 1790s at the same time as larger numbers of Appalachian Scots-Irish crossed the Pennsylvania and Virginia borders.

As settlement swelled, Ohio's population jumped from 230,000 in 1810—Shawnee and Wyandot war parties still prowled the state's northwest—to some 900,000 in 1830. A further flood more than doubled the population to nearly 2 million in 1850. Ohio became to the canal, steamboat, and Conestoga wagon era what California would be to the automobile and airplane in the decades after World War II: not just a beacon but a national symbol of westward migration.

"The immigration to the North Central section," concluded historian Frederick Jackson Turner, "had a special significance. In the Atlantic states, from the colonial days, the rule of the older stock was well-established, and institutions, manners and customs—the cultural life of the sections—had been largely fixed by tradition. But in the New West, society was plastic and democratic. All elements were suddenly coming in, together, to form the section. It would be a mistake to think that social classes and distinctions were obliterated, but in general, no such stratification existed as was to be found, especially, in New England."[1]

Buckeye agriculture complemented Jacksonian democracy, being small-holder based and a far cry from plantations of the Cotton South or the quasi-feudal land holdings of New York's Hudson Valley. Farmers were lured by the fifty to sixty bushels an acre corn yields of the fertile Muskingum, Scioto, and Miami valleys, two or three times what they could grow on hillside or tidewater plots back east. By the 1840s, two extensive state-built waterways connected Ohio farmlands to Lake Erie and the Erie Canal, opening up the Eastern U.S. and European corn and wheat markets. Higher crop prices followed.

Additional help came from the reaper and other new farm machinery. In 1840, Ohio was the leading wheat-producing state ranked by yield. This slipped to second in 1850 and fourth in 1860 as the grain belt moved west.[2] In corn, however, Ohio had been fourth in 1840, but rose to first place in 1850. Corn was marketed largely on the hoof—cattle and hogs fed on it, then were slaughtered, packed, and sent east or abroad.

Not surprisingly, Ohio led the nation in livestock in 1850. Meat-packing Cincinnati had already won the nickname "Porkopolis," and Ohio's sheep-raising eastern counties likewise made it the number one wool-raising state. A century later, one would err taking Ohio as the heart of the Farm Belt, but not in the years of McKinley's boyhood.

Biblical land of Goshen as the state might seem, abundant crops did not always lead to prosperity. That had been proved in the late 1830s and 1840s when banks failed and low meat and grain prices barely exceeded production costs. Prosperity returned in the 1850s, but by the late sixties and early seventies, Washington's acquiescence in a post–Civil War contraction of the currency was provoking crop and livestock districts alike.

As president, McKinley would fondly reminisce about how, as a barefoot nine-year-old, he took his family's cows to and from pasture. Yet from the start, his part of Ohio was also industrial. At the time of McKinley's birth, the *Niles Tribune-Chronicle* later recalled, the town had included "3 churches, 3 stores, 1 blast furnace, rolling mill, nail factory forge and about 300 inhabitants."[3] Even in 1820, only Pennsylvania and New York surpassed Ohio in the value of manufactured goods, and this kind of interspersed small-scale industry characterized the Ohio countryside until the Civil War.

McKinley's grandfather James, and his father, William, were iron makers by trade. In the early nineteenth century, they came to Ohio from Pennsylvania, where Scots-Irish iron masters, aroused by prohibitions in the British Iron Act of 1750 against colonials making pig iron into ironware and machinery, had been a mainstay of the American Revolution. In 1804, Daniel Heaton built Ohio's first smelting furnace on Yellow Creek, near the present site of Youngstown. This was the forerunner of the Mahoning Valley steel industry, at its twentieth-century peak second only to that of nearby Pittsburgh.

Iron quickly became Ohio's leading manufacturing industry, with the 1850 census ranking state pig-iron output second only to Pennsylvania's. Coal and iron production both concentrated in the eastern counties where the McKinleys always had a small furnace or two.

Turnpikes, canals, and railroads crisscrossed the area where McKinley grew up. By the 1850s, the railroad concentrations of northeastern Ohio rivaled those centered on Boston, New York, and Philadelphia.[4] At the Civil War's outbreak, Ohio led the nation in railroad mileage, and when Buckeye soldiers got leave, all they had to do was reach the Baltimore & Ohio line in the east or the Louisville & Cincinnati in the west. Home would be only hours away.

Like Ohio's centrality in late-nineteenth-century politics, its significance to U.S. manufacturing is hard to exaggerate. Between young Will McKinley's birth and his election to the presidency in 1896, the state's industrial innovation was the stuff of record books—literally.

Cleveland had John D. Rockefeller at work in the Ohio oilfields and refinery district, as well as Charles Brush, whose invention of the arc light illuminated America's cities. Young Thomas A. Edison spent some of his boyhood puttering in the town of Milan. Charles Martin Hall, based in Oberlin, in 1886 discovered the electrolytic process for making aluminum. Toledo to the northwest claimed Edward Libbey and Michael Owens, whose inventions and local company, Libby-Owens-Ford, revolutionized the glass and bottle business.

Dayton boasted the Wright brothers, who tinkered with the forerunners of flying machines in their local bicycle shop, as well as the Patterson brothers who started National Cash Register in 1884. The inventions of Charles Kettering, who started Delco, ranged from electric starters for automobiles to the iron lung. Fifty miles to the south, candle molder William Procter and soap maker James Gamble were already building the company that eventually made Cincinnati a household-product word.

In McKinley's own backyard, B. F. Goodrich and Harvey Firestone made Akron the rubber capital of the world in the 1870s and 1880s. The National Inventor's Hall of Fame, located there, has been described by the *Wall Street Journal* as "a Cooperstown for gadgeteers and tinkerers." The Studebaker brothers grew up in Wooster before building their cars. J. Ward Packard produced electrical equipment in Warren before putting his name on a luxury automobile.

Few remember Joshua Gibbs, whose newfangled iron plows turned Canton, Ohio, into the nation's leading pre–Civil War producer of farm machinery. Without that base, the city might not have lured youthful lawyer McKinley in 1869. William H. Hoover developed the vacuum cleaner, and his company remains a Canton institution.

Small wonder that innovation became part of McKinley's argument for the protective system. "It encourages the development of skill and inventive genius as part of the great productive forces," he said as a young man awed by what he saw around him. He identified the tariff with national development and patriotism, and, in the words of biographer H. Wayne Morgan, "through the dull tax [tariff] schedules that bored other men, he found the romance of history in the unfolding development of the nation's wealth."[5]

The best parallel is to the Britain of 1750 to 1820, with its early Industrial Revolution convergence of communications, foundries, factories, and, most of all, innovations. The most notable were James Hargreaves's spinning jenny (1766), James Watt's steam engine (1768), Henry Cort's patents for puddling and rolling iron (1783–84), and Richard Arkwright's power loom (1787). Like post–Civil War Ohio, early industrial Britain had secured and mobilized itself with tariffs, strict patent laws, government assistance, and military procurement, as well as the Navigation Acts that gave preference to British shipping and parliamentary statutes that sought to prohibit skilled workers and engineers from leaving the country.

Born and bred in such innovative surroundings, McKinley's speeches about enterprise and the fruits of the protective tariff system often sounded trite, like paeans from a chamber of commerce brochure. But they had a base in reality. When he came home from the war, factories belched smoke where only a few sheep had grazed. A decade later, when Rutherford Hayes recommended that the new congressman hook his career to a specialty in tariffs, McKinley's own district was practically a casebook; witness the 1860 to 1900 population explosion in three of its manufacturing cities: Youngstown—2500 percent, Akron—1300 percent, Canton—1200 percent.

However, if Ohio politics and commerce were powerful in molding McKinley, so were two other home-state institutions: the Methodist Church and Abraham Lincoln's boys in blue, the Ohio Volunteers and the Grand Army of the Republic.

OHIO AS THE NINETEENTH-CENTURY MIDDLE AMERICA

The Ohio of McKinley's youth reflected the just-past-the-frontier culture of the burgeoning Midwest: a new unpolished middle class given to teetotaling Methodism, religious camp meetings, and small-town values, typically light-years distant from the sophistication of upper-class Eastern universities, salons, and clubs.

Some biographers have dealt condescendingly with his midwestern manners, his fondness for homilies, his open religiosity, his middle-class taste, his unflagging commitment to "the people," and a liking for popular hymns, sentimental poetry, and patriotic odes. His devotion to his invalid wife, counted entirely genuine even by foes, drew a certain mockery for its Victorian syrup of language and expression, including gestures like his effort as governor always to wave to her window at three o'clock in the afternoon.

These attributes, however, also had a positive effect: they helped to give William McKinley, Jr., the greatest personal popularity of any president since Lincoln. His success on the stump, his ability to draw crowds everywhere, and his obvious personal following would be used to rebuild executive power that a generation of lesser presidents—some able to read Kant or Plutarch in the original—had lost to Congress. In late-nineteenth-century politics, his personality was a pillar of his success, whatever disdain it might evoke among later sophisticates.

Religiosity was part of that drawing power. In eighteenth-century Pennsylvania, the McKinleys had been Scots-Irish Presbyterians committed to kirk and covenant. But not long after arriving in Ohio, they became Methodists, caught up in the revivalism of the early nineteenth century. By 1844, when the Methodist Church divided between north and south, Methodism had become America's most popular creed, with over a million members and almost twelve thousand local and itinerant preachers.[6] This itinerant capacity, together with emphasis on camp meetings—so named for the tents that provided early housing—particularly equipped the Methodists to evangelize a moving frontier.

Ohio was one of their strongholds, and among those recruited to atonement, grace, and the sanctifying work of the Holy Spirit was young Will McKinley, who requested baptism after a series of camp meetings in 1859. His mother hoped his commitment would lead him to the ministry, but the Civil War intervened. Still, his regiment—the Twenty-third Ohio Volunteer Infantry, to whom we shall return shortly—was scarcely less religious than his home environs. Nicknamed "the psalm-singers of the Western Reserve," they followed a routine he described to his sister as "religious exercises in the company twice a day, prayer meetings twice a week, and preaching in the regiment once on a sabbath."[7]

As the war lengthened and McKinley rose in rank, he gave up his 1861 habit of referring to himself as a soldier of Jesus, as well as of the North. Even so, religion remained prominent in his speech. As president, his addresses would be sprinkled with phrases like the Lord Most High and Him who is a sovereign of land and sea. In fact, this was common for post–Civil War presidents. James Garfield, as a member of Congress, averted an April 1865 riot in New York City with a biblical invocation: "Mercy and truth shall go before His face. Fellow Citizens! God reigns and the Government at Washington still lives."[8] Louis Auchincloss has pointed out that Theodore Roosevelt, a half century later, "could speak of standing at Armageddon to do battle for the Lord without being laughed off the platform."[9]

McKinley's first minister, Aaron Morton, said he "was not what you would call a 'shouting Methodist,' but rather one who was careful of his acts and words. . . ."[10] Upon moving from the Western Reserve several dozen miles south to Canton in 1867, he became president of the local YMCA and stressed devotion, not denomination, gathering young men of every faith for song and prayer.

> His devout Methodism did not lead him to concern himself with dogma or denominational differences. The loving kindness of God was McKinley's religion, and the source of his inner serenity. . . . He made many friends among Canton's large Roman Catholic population of German and Irish extraction. In a day of sharp sectarianism, McKinley was devoid of bigotry possessing as a grace of his nature the tolerance that is unconscious of its own virtue.[11]

Canton and Stark County were more ecumenical than the nearby Western Reserve. Together with the adjacent counties to the east, west, and south, they were Ohio's principal "Little Pennsylvania," with a religious heterogeneity to match that which had made William Penn's Philadelphia the center of eighteenth-century North American toleration. Denominational maps of Ohio in 1850 and 1890 show the counties in McKinley's congressional district with major concentrations of Methodists, Catholics, Lutherans, German Reformed, Presbyterians, Amish, Mennonites, United Brethren, Disciples of Christ, and Quakers. Toleration was almost a necessity.

Pundits of a later date might have called McKinley "Middle American," and indeed, if the antebellum United States had a Middle America, it was the Buckeye State. Ohio straddled an extended Mason-Dixon Line in both physical geography and mixed Northern-Southern antecedents. Poland, where McKinley lived as a teenager, was a Yankee settlement—replete with a New England town green and several academies—on the southern edge of what had once been Connecticut's Western Reserve. But it was only twenty miles to the northern loop of the Ohio River, on the other side of which was slaveholding Virginia.

Ohio also stood between the old and more stratified Atlantic coastal sections and the Wisconsin-Iowa-Missouri frontier, and was also middling in respect for the political and economic values of the Eastern elites. Outside of a few university towns, high culture was not an Ohio aspiration. Remarks about effete Easterners were common and occasionally indulged in by the McKinley family.

Politically, the McKinleys were Western Whigs, a different breed from their Eastern compatriots. When Ohio's William Henry Harrison, scion of an old Southern family, ran as the Whig nominee for president in 1840, he paraded under a banner of log cabins and hard cider. Another local Whig, U.S. Senator Thomas Corwin, took political, if not personal, pleasure in his nickname "the Wagon Boy." Even Garfield, who went East to college, would later be portrayed as a youthful hauler on the ropes of canal boats.

Midcentury Ohio did not have a refined or bookish culture, and some chroniclers have mistakenly dismissed McKinley's literacy as well as his taste. Margaret Leech, a generally esteeming biographer, nevertheless stated: "He had few intellectual resources. If he had ever possessed a germ of taste, it died of inanition. In literature and music, he looked for an obvious sentimental, patriotic or religious content." Worse, by the time he was in his forties, "with the passing years, McKinley's desire to improve his mind became scarcely more than lip service to a recollected aspiration. After he was elected governor of Ohio, he read two books that [Myron] Herrick sent him as a Christmas present. There is no other mention of his reading, apart from the newspapers."[12]

This is simply untrue, and condescending as well as pedantic. "Inanition," so the dictionary says, means "emptiness, exhaustion from hunger"—from the Latin *inanis*. Twenty-one years later, biographer Lewis Gould would better describe McKinley's habits: "[H]e frequently read late into the night. Novels, works of history and the endless reports were his reading materials. McKinley was far more bookish and better informed than his reputation as a non-reading president would seem to indicate."[13]

Indeed, Leech's dismissal of his reading follows only two dozen pages after a kindred opening. She begins her biography in 1896 with the governor of Ohio returning to Canton after two successful terms, happily coming back to his former house on North Market Street—a midsized white frame structure of no particular cachet. His chosen furnishings included a worn but reupholstered lounge, an old McKinley favorite, for his library. Newly added was an elaborately carved sitting-room table made from many different Ohio woods—maple, hop hornbeam, oak, wild cherry, hickory, poplar, sassafras, among others—that "he had set his heart on owning" after seeing it at the 1893 Chicago World's Fair. "In all America," the author confides, "there was no mansion so fine and costly that it was to be compared in McKinley's mind with that snug cottage on North Market Street."[14]

This snub may be fair culturally—McKinley obviously didn't know a Hepplewhite from a Chippendale—but it is unsophisticated politically. Then as now, voters warm to an honest and effective public servant who'd rather live on middle-class Main Street with a devoted spouse than discuss Tolstoy in fashionable salons.

Perhaps more to the point, inasmuch as visitors to nineteenth-century Ohio found even the local middle-class literati stylistically wanting, the lack of style must have extended beyond McKinley. English writer Frances Trollope, after her 1830 visit to Cincinnati, reported that Ohio writers were inferior and "the style of their imaginative compositions was almost always affected and inflated."[15] Ohio novelist William Dean Howells, a contemporary of McKinley who published *The Hazard of New Fortunes* to considerable acclaim in 1890, received a kindred review a century later on his book's reissuance. Howells's characters, said the critic, "remain unimagined; and in an odd way, so does the prose."

If McKinley's taste and prose failed to rise to athenaeum standards, it is not so easy to dismiss his intelligence. As governor and president, he often avoided setting out his policy views, but the frequent shrewdness of this tactic will be amplified in chapter 6. Putdowns of his vocabulary also seem tenuous. The language he employed during his career was simple; its uncomplicated directness had been honed in wartime military correspondence and in persuading Stark County jurors who might have spurned a lawyer given to grandiloquent displays. Moreover, a quick scanning of excerpts from the diary that eighteen-year-old Private Will McKinley kept for six months in 1861 turns up words like "oblivious," "weltering," "literati," and "accoutrements." Presumably he had not yet developed a need to think in terms of juries and electorates.

Although neither abstraction nor dense literature held much appeal to him, he was a quick study. One grade-school teacher required him to sit up front "in order to give other students a chance to plod through what he seemed to learn at a glance."[16] John Hay, his secretary of state, recalled after McKinley's death that "He had an extraordinary power of marshaling and presenting significant facts, so as to bring conviction to the average mind. His range of reading was not wide; he read only what he might some day find useful, and what he read his memory held like brass."[17]

Until recently, the McKinley of 1861 to 1865 did not have a separate biographer, a gap filled in 2000 by William Armstrong's *Major McKinley: William McKinley and the Civil War.* Before he went off to fight after just a few months of college, the eighteen-year-old had always been interested in books and reading material. His father had left such things to his mother, who wanted her son to be a churchman, "and the McKinley home received some of the best periodicals of the time: the *Atlantic Monthly* (young Will McKinley's favorite), *Harper's Monthly*, and Horace Greeley's *New York Weekly Tribune.* Each evening, the family gathered in the sitting room where they spent an hour taking turns reading aloud."[18] William McKinley, Sr., to be sure, often preferred the earthier writings of fellow Scotsman Robert Burns.

In 1852, when William was nine, the family moved to nearby Poland, which had a private academy the children could attend. Persevering and diligent, he did well, and after graduation in 1860 went off to Allegheny College, a hundred miles away in Meadville, Pennsylvania. He soon left and came home, as he recalled, because of a nervous condition that turned into depression.[19] His father's subsequent business failure kept him from returning to college after his condition improved, so he taught school, worked in the post office, and in June of 1861, after careful consideration, responded to Lincoln's call for volunteers. In Poland's Old Stone Tavern, a Pittsburgh-Cleveland stage stop that dated back to 1804, he enlisted for three years as a private in the Poland Guards, a company filled with his schoolmates. He would get his education, cum laude, in the War for the Preservation of the Union.

MCKINLEY AND THE CIVIL WAR

Mustered in at Ohio's Camp Jackson, McKinley soon gave up the book of Byron's poems he had brought along for the more pertinent pages of *Hardee's Tactics*—a military manual written by an ex-officer in the U.S. Army turned Confederate general. As the appointed "correspondent" of the Poland Guards company, Private McKinley began writing letters that were published in the Mahoning *Register,* the newspaper in nearby Youngstown. He wrote to his sister that "the (mealtime) mess which I am in is composed principally of the *literati* of the company."[20] However, they were soon too busy chasing Confederates around divided West Virginia to do more than read four-day-old newspapers and posted telegraph dispatches. He stopped keeping his diary in November 1861, when he was made quartermaster clerk. He still tried to read on quiet Sundays.

In April 1862, Private McKinley was promoted to the rank of quartermaster sergeant, which required that he keep the regiment provisioned and fed. Come summer, his unit moved to Washington, D.C. On the fourteenth of September, the Ohio Division, with his Twenty-third Regiment out in front, marched along the National Road toward South Mountain in western Maryland, eventually making a successful charge to clear away the Confederates holding the hilltop.

Three days later and a dozen miles farther west, the Twenty-third fought again in the battle of Antietam. Having crossed Antietam Creek, several units were cut off. The nineteen-year-old McKinley, as acting commissary, wanted to get food to the trapped men. He went back behind the lines, rounded up stragglers, and put them to work preparing food and hot coffee. When it was ready, he loaded a wagon, asked for a volunteer to go with him, and prepared to ride through an open field controlled by Confederate fire. As he approached, two officers told him to retire because it was impossible. He went anyway and got through, despite the rear of the wagon being taken off by a small cannonball.

When the Twenty-third again suffered heavy casualties, its

commander, Colonel Rutherford B. Hayes, the future president, recommended McKinley for a vacant lieutenancy, and he received the commission personally from Ohio Governor David Tod in November. In January 1863, Hayes, now commanding a brigade of Ohioans, made Lieutenant McKinley the brigade quartermaster, supervising clerks, a carpenter, a forage master, a wagon master, a harness master, two blacksmiths, and five teamsters. When he had free time on Sundays, he read histories and biographies of military men, and Colonel Hayes augmented McKinley's library with a personally inscribed copy of Silas Casey's *Tactics*.

Many of the men from northern Ohio, knowing only their flat homelands, filled pages of their diaries with awed descriptions of the West Virginia mountains. Ambrose Bierce, serving in another regiment, later recalled, "I note again their dim, blue billows, ridge after ridge interminable, beyond purple valleys full of sleep."[21] McKinley, though, was now too busy with practical matters—requisitions, forms, and ledgers—to go back to his own diary. His future bent for facts and statistics was unfolding.

Stationed in West Virginia through most of 1863, the Twenty-third saw no major battles, but participated in a number of lesser actions. One successfully ended the last days of Confederate cavalry leader John Morgan's famous raid into Ohio. In January 1864, Lieutenant McKinley became the assistant adjutant general of Hayes's brigade, which for the invasion of Virginia was assigned to the division commanded by General George Crook, later a famous Indian fighter. At the battle of Kernstown, McKinley rode through enemy-held positions and shot and shell to give orders to a reserve regiment about to be overrun. He was promoted to captain, and Crook thereupon took him as one of his adjutants in what soon became the Army of West Virginia, part of Philip H. Sheridan's larger Army of the Shenandoah.

At the battle of Berryville in September 1864, McKinley had a horse shot from under him, and two weeks later, Sheridan and Crook sent McKinley with a message for the commander of the Second Division to bring those troops up to the line. That officer said he would take the recommended route only if ordered by General Crook, at which point Captain McKinley straightened in his saddle and said, "Then by order of General Crook, I command you."[22] Crook accepted his aide's initiative, but had it failed, McKinley would have been in trouble.

Sheridan credited Crook with turning the tide in the battles of Winchester and Fisher's Hill. McKinley, in turn, was recognized in Crook's own report. Staff officers riding to and fro had a high rate of attrition, and in the words of one, they felt "they carried their lives in their hands as well as their dispatches, and if a twig cracked by the roadside, it seemed ominous of bullets and sudden death."[23]

At the battle of Cedar Creek, when a returning Sheridan made his famous "wild ride" to rally demoralized Union troops, McKinley, now a brevet major, played a role, as Sheridan recalled in his later *Memoirs.* Others said that when Sheridan determined to make the ride, it was the young Ohio major who suggested that the general take off his plain overcoat and put on the epaulets that the weary men would recognize.

By this point, McKinley was the chief adjutant in the field with the Army of West Virginia. On Election Day, November 8, 1864, he issued orders for Crook's corps to join the rest of Sheridan's army in moving back to Kernstown. Then, at age twenty-one, he voted in his first presidential election at the army ambulance that was the polling place of the Thirty-fourth Ohio Infantry. The men who voted with him were Rutherford Hayes, George Crook, and Philip H. Sheridan.

By the spring of 1865, he was serving as divisional adjutant and chief of staff for a new unit under Major General Samuel S. Carroll. But three days after he joined the division at Winchester, Robert E. Lee surrendered. McKinley's Civil War was over, and although he thought about staying in the army—a peacetime lieutenancy was offered—he ultimately chose not to do so.

Not surprisingly, he never went back to Allegheny College. His only further education was a term at Albany Law School in New York, following a year in Ohio reading law with Judge Charles Glidden. Despite his complaints at having to learn "the old customs of the Saxons and the Danes," the months in Albany were bearable, because his was a "war class" said to include veterans of every rank from major general down to private.[24] The twenty-three-year-old ex-major would not have stood out.

Murat Halstead, a well-known journalist and eventual McKinley biographer, opined that "the [military] camp was to him a university. . . . When the combat closed, Major McKinley was an officer and a gentleman, who had built in his diversified education wiser than he knew, and taken a degree beyond any the colleges could confer."[25]

If anything, this is an understatement, given McKinley's shoulder rubbing with men who managed the greatest crisis of nineteenth-century America. Beside their state's role as a Midwest pivot, part of why Ohioans commanded the mountaintop of national and Republican politics in the half century after Appomattox involved the bonds of their wartime service. Politics in the Midwest had been forged by the war and would divide over its memories for decades. Just as the North's military success was marshaled by the Ohio-born Grant, Sherman, and Sheridan, the Republican Party dominated post–Civil War presidential politics in fair measure by nominating Ohioans with battlefield as well as geographic credentials.

This network would be invaluable to McKinley, who began his political career in 1867 campaigning up and down Stark County for the gubernatorial candidacy of his regimental commander, Rutherford Hayes. After Hayes won, McKinley became the Republican county chairman in Stark and organized the county for Grant's 1868 presidential campaign. The Twenty-third Regiment itself was already an incalculably more important fraternity for McKinley than the Sigma Alpha Epsilon he had briefly joined in 1860.

This one volunteer regiment, with its long casualty list and high reputation, produced two Ohio governors, Hayes and McKinley, who went on to become presidents; two lieutenant governors of Ohio, Robert P. Kennedy and William C. Lyon; four U.S. congressmen, Hayes, McKinley, Kennedy, and William S. Rosecrans; and a U.S. senator who later became an associate justice of the U.S. Supreme Court, Stanley Matthews.[26] With such attendees, the annual reunions of the Twenty-third often also drew visiting vice presidents, war secretaries, and House speakers.

Both Hayes and McKinley professed to be prouder of those days and the cause they fought for than anything else they did in their lives. Oliver Wendell Holmes, Jr., said of that same 1861–65 service that "Through our great fortune, in our youth our hearts were touched with fire." Despite their later offices, Hayes liked to be addressed as "Colonel" and McKinley as "Major." Both rarely missed regimental reunions and were almost always available to fellow veterans who wanted to see them. Part of what seems to have inspired the two future presidents to the commitments of their careers was a sense of how much the United States owed to their comrades in arms from the Twenty-third who never lived to farm a hundred acres outside Canton, teach at Poland Academy, or represent Trumbull County in the state legislature.

THE TRIBULATIONS OF A RISING POLITICIAN

The first elected office McKinley held was that of Stark County prosecutor, which he won in 1869 somewhat by accident, given Stark's Democratic bias. He failed by a small margin when he sought a second term in 1871. However, his law practice did well, and Governor Hayes was both an ally and a mentor. In 1876, Hayes, as a surprise presidential nominee, carried Ohio but became president only by a one-vote national electoral vote majority arranged through an unseemly North-South political bargain. This haunted Hayes's single, essentially unsuccessful term. That same year, McKinley won a seat in Congress. His district included Stark, Mahoning, and Columbiana counties, a politically marginal stretch of grainfields, coal mines, iron furnaces, and potteries.

For reasons beyond politics, though, the new congressman left for Washington in 1877 with a heavy heart. Six years earlier, at twenty-eight, he had married Ida Saxton, the very pretty but high-strung daughter of one of Canton's most prominent families. Their first child, Katie, arrived in December 1871. The next little girl came in 1873, on a day when Ida McKinley, almost simultaneously stricken by news of her own mother's death, underwent a hard and traumatic labor. The new baby died five months later. Ida McKinley herself developed convulsions that suggested brain damage. She became an epileptic with seizures.

In the summer of 1876, just before McKinley won his House seat, Katie, the daughter who looked so much like her father, also died. These tragedies altered him, biographer Leech concluded. "His buoyant youthfulness was gone. He showed the fortitude and quick compassion that are the grace of those who have greatly suffered, but he also grew guarded and reticent. In the first shock of his trouble, he was sometimes abstracted. There were stories that he forgot important testimony that had been given in court; that his intense gaze became a fixed stare, as though he were mustering all his faculties in an effort at concentration."[27] If McKinley had left college years earlier because of depression, the trauma of the years 1873 to 1876 may have partially reshaped his personality.

The grief-stricken Ohioan was not an ordinary new congressman. He was a protégé of the new president, despite Hayes's disputed election and minimal standing in Congress. He and Ida saw much of the White House. Although Hayes went back to Ohio after four years, ironically, the 1880 GOP national convention picked a second Ohioan as a compromise nominee after multiple ballots. This one was James A. Garfield, a fellow House member, who sometimes brought his sons to call on the McKinleys at Washington's Ebbitt House. Six months later, he fell to an assassin's bullet.

Hard work in Congress helped to take McKinley's mind off his pain, but his wife's needs took up most of his evenings. "He was tireless," says Leech, "in ministering to her mental and physical comfort. He grew soft-voiced and cautious, and developed resources of tact. . . . He turned an imperturbable face to the pitying eyes of Canton, and his reserve forbade impertinent questioning. In the presence of other people, McKinley's attitude toward Ida's repellent symptoms [facial convulsions] was so casual as to appear indifferent. He always sat beside her in the dining room or parlor. At the first sign of rigidity, he was alert. He threw his handkerchief or a napkin over her convulsed face, removing it when she relaxed. McKinley's matter-of-fact manner forbade a whisper of comment."[28]

Cautiousness, refusal to explain or discuss unpleasantness, and a skill in pleasing people were traits McKinley learned during these years and would display through his political career. All too often, such characteristics would be cited to support accusations of weakness, mediocrity, indecision, and seeming dependence on the direction of others. So described, they have plagued his historical memory. At the time, contrarily, these skills helped him win friends, and large numbers of Americans in Ohio and elsewhere came to admire the congressman for the time and attention he devoted to his wife. Julia Foraker, the wife of one of McKinley's home-state rivals, would later contend that it was the key to his popularity and success.

In any event, these circumstances did nothing to slow down his rise in Congress or national politics. We will look at the tariff issue in chapter 2 and his political rise in chapter 3. However, Ohio Democrats, recognizing him as one of the state's rising Republican stars, sought to defeat him. They spent the decade after 1881 gerrymandering McKinley's congressional district whenever they controlled the legislature, attaching his home county of Stark to different sets of adjacent counties. He kept coming back.

Year after year, meanwhile, he saw men born in Ohio win the presidency—Hayes in 1876, Garfield in 1880, Harrison in 1888. Still another Ohioan, U.S. Senator John Sherman, had been an important contender in the Republican presidential nomination contests from 1880 to 1888, although he never won. No other state could have opened such a large window into such high-level national politics, and McKinley took full advantage of his education, both in state and national politics and in the legislating processes of Congress.

In 1889, he came within one vote of being chosen by his party as Speaker of the House of Representatives. The winner, Thomas Brackett Reed of Maine, thereupon appointed McKinley as chair man of the Ways and Means Committee and Republican floor leader. The irony was that the congressman from Canton was finally about to return home. Put back in control of the Ohio legislature in 1889, the Democrats drew yet another new Eighteenth Congressional District for 1890. This gerrymander pulled McKinley south and west into areas largely settled by Pennsylvania Germans who disliked the Civil War and voted heavily Democratic. Previous remappings had failed to achieve the Democrats' projected vote totals, but this time they inserted one of their two best Ohio counties— Holmes. Civil War buffs will remember "Fort Fizzle," scene of the 1863 "Holmes County Rebellion," described in one local history:

> When the draft act was passed, many people protested. In Democratic Holmes County a recruiting officer was stoned and his life threatened. When four men were arrested for this

attack, a group of residents attempted to secure their release by intimidating the military commander of the district. Finally the military sent a force of 450 soldiers to Glenmont, from which place they marched to a fortified camp nearby. Here 900 men armed with guns and several howitzers awaited them behind a stone barrier in a large orchard. After a few shots were fired the fractious rebels fled; the incident was settled by negotiation, and a few indictments were returned. Colonel Wallace was said to have dubbed the spot Fort Fizzle.[29]

Interpretations of the election outcome in 1890 depend on one's viewpoint. The Democratic legislature's projected majority of three thousand never materialized, even in a year devastating to the Republicans nationally. McKinley fought hard, losing by only three hundred votes. The state's Republican newspapers hailed his moral victory in a nest of copperheads, as wartime Southern sympathizers were called. They proclaimed him the logical party nominee and near-certain winner in the upcoming 1891 gubernatorial election. Some predicted that Ohio would soon put another Republican in the White House. The final volley from Fort Fizzle was the last election William McKinley would ever lose.

2

Surprisingly Modern McKinley

On the great new questions as they arose, he [McKinley] was generally on the side of the public against private interests.
                                    Senator Robert La Follette, *Memoirs*

As an ally of McKinley in the House Ways and Means Committee
and later in 1896 presidential nominating politics, La Follette knew
him better than most. Mark Hanna added that whereas he and
the president were both of Scots-Irish descent, Hanna had the Irish
traits—outgoing, outspoken, happiest in convivial company.
McKinley, who kept his own counsel, was the circumspect, deliber-
ate Scot.[1] His success with numbers, management, and people
made him a good twenty-year-old army adjutant, a capable thirty-
year-old lawyer, and a well-versed forty-five-year-old Washington
tariff policy maker and debater. Yet his circumspection also seems
to have cloaked viewpoints more on the modern (and sometimes
radical) side than his corporate and Methodist Sunday school image
implied.

The Scottish heritage of William McKinley, Sr., coupled with his
taste for the writings of Burns, may have helped to imbue the
younger William with his enthusiasm for democracy, equality, and
labor rights, a modest late-century Ohio reprise of the spirit of
Burns's famous poem "For 'a that and a' that." Indeed, as president,
McKinley did once dismiss "ribbons, stars, and a' that," refusing to
let the army go forward in awarding him a Congressional Medal of
Honor for bravery three decades earlier during the Civil War. Even
as congressman, governor, and president, he liked being called by
his Civil War rank. "How shall I address you?" one fellow veteran of

the Twenty-third asked him after the 1896 election. "Call me Major," he said. "I earned that. I am not so sure of the rest."[2]

In 1876, as a young lawyer, he had volunteered to defend striking coal miners although friends said it would hurt him politically. As a congressman, although pressed by expenses, he repeatedly spurned highly paid job offers from corporations and refused speaking fees. He quietly favored women's suffrage. In cities like Cincinnati and New Orleans, he changed hotels when they would not admit blacks with whom he was to meet. He sought the 1896 Republican presidential nomination as the candidate of "the people" after refusing to make a deal with the powerful GOP bosses of New York and Pennsylvania, Thomas Platt and Matthew Quay. Wisconsin's Robert La Follette, later a famous Progressive, saw much of the same in McKinley.

Administratively, he was the first president to make extensive use of the telephone, to develop systematized press operations, to have a news summary, and to make the White House a news center. National politics, for better or worse, was beginning its transformation into commercial marketing. Theodore Roosevelt commented that the Republican National Committee in 1896 sold McKinley like soap, and it was during McKinley's first term that the national party inaugurated the use of Victrola devices to make the recorded comments of senators and congressmen available to their constituencies. The Spanish-American War, in turn, became the first to be managed from a White House war room connected to military headquarters in Washington and the field by telephone and telegraph.

Extensive travel became another hallmark. He was the first incumbent president to visit California. Before his assassination in 1901, McKinley was planning trips that would have made him the first incumbent to travel abroad. This, he thought, befitted the new status of the United States as a world power.

Much about the twenty-fifth president, in short, did not fit his stereotype. Many historians have taken his lack of personal papers and discursive private letters, together with his tendency to listen as much as talk, as proof of mediocrity and other-directedness. Others have noted, in the words of one, that "the minds of few public men have been so well concealed."[3] The case for his unappreciated mastery of communications—employing personal openness, press relations, marketing techniques, highly effective speeches, and autumn Republican campaign swings—is supported by his suasion in Washington and national politics. He achieved quite a lot, often without presenting much of a target.

His broad philosophic leanings can be gleaned from home-state alliances and circumstances. In Ohio politics, he identified with the moderately reformist camp that also included Hayes, Garfield, and John Sherman. Their broadly shared positions included a relative ecumenicalism on religious and ethnic issues, greater acceptance of labor unions and railroad regulation than prevailed among Eastern conservatives, support for civil service reform, and opposition to the national party influence and patronage demands of the Eastern state GOP machine leaders. With Sherman, the Ohio party's grand old man, McKinley also shared a periodic willingness to compromise money issues of gold versus silver. More than the other three, however, McKinley represented a commitment to the people and their rule, the "touch of Lincoln" that Midwest Republicans of that era thought so effective.

Like the sixteenth president, his sympathy for enterprise and tariff protection hinged more on its upholding of labor than of capital. Unlike Theodore Roosevelt, McKinley never directly repeated and approved Lincoln's comments about labor being more deserving than capital. But for those who paid close attention, his actions spoke louder than his careful words.

LABOR AND CAPITAL IN OHIO

During McKinley's boyhood, his father managed an iron furnace in Niles, a task described by one early biographer as requiring "a strong physique and skill of many and varied kinds . . . the duties of the manager included the chopping of wood, the burning of the charcoal, the mining of the ore and all the details of the manufacture of the resultant product, pig iron."[4] Up to the Civil War, physical work and a return on (small) capital went together across most of Ohio, large industrial works being uncommon.

Abraham Lincoln absorbed much the same ethos in 1840s Illinois. Midwesterners distrusted nonlaboring capital of the detached, Eastern sort. Antibank riots have enlivened Ohio in the 1820s, and

William Henry Harrison, a local state senator before he became president, responded by saying that he would like to see all banks destroyed, if that were possible. He even came out for using tax policy to drive the local branch of the Bank of the United States out of the state.[5] Wary of reliance on private institutions, the Ohio legislation set up the State Bank of Ohio, with seventeen branches, to guide a system which also included nine so-called independent banks.[6]

Labor unions got an early toehold, although membership rose and fell with the economy. By 1830, Cincinnati had the first city federation of unions west of Philadelphia. Two decades later, the city's printers formed what Ohioans claim as the first permanent national labor union. The American Federation of Labor got its start in an 1886 assemblage in Columbus, which chose Samuel Gompers as president. Three years later, another meeting in Columbus launched the United Mine Workers of America.[7]

In next-door Pennsylvania, by contrast, the mine-district terrorism of the 1860s by the Molly Maguires led to the creation of Pennsylvania's infamous Iron and Coal Police and the use of Pinkerton agents as strikebreakers. Local sentiment in Ohio often supported the miners in strikes, with businessmen and store owners trying to help.

Popular sentiment was less than friendly, though, in the Stark County town of Massillon, in June 1876, when thirty-three coal miners were imprisoned for rioting during a violent strike. McKinley nevertheless chose to defend them and got all but one set free. When their friends pulled together the money to pay their young lawyer, he declined to take it. Thus began his strong labor support and eventual electoral invulnerability in his home county.

McKinley maintained that connection in Congress, proposing in 1886 a national system of arbitration of labor disputes, a system shortly thereafter pioneered at the state level in Massachusetts. After his election as governor in 1891, McKinley made Ohio the second state to establish arbitration. As governor, he also brought about laws to protect railroad and streetcar employees from accident and exposure and, more boldly, to fine employers who prevented their workers from joining unions. Sympathetic biographer H. Wayne Morgan ranked labor as his state administration's "chief concern . . . his interest reflected his career as a labor lawyer, his understanding of labor's growing strength and changing status, and his sympathy with the working man's problems."[8]

The sympathies of McKinley and other Midwestern governors were tested during the economic depression from 1893 to 1894. In the late spring of 1894, striking Ohio coal miners, infuriated by shipments of "scab" Virginia and West Virginia coal carried by the Toledo & Ohio Central Railroad, destroyed a T&OC trestle in southern Ohio's Hocking Valley. At the local sheriff's request, Governor McKinley sent in militia, but it turned out that local officials had exaggerated. The soldiers were withdrawn, and the miners adopted a resolution finding McKinley blameless.[9] Then the situation worsened. At first, McKinley refused troops, but on June 2, after the miners farther north seized coal trains coming from West Virginia, McKinley did send in the army—regiment upon regiment, even artillery, totaling 3,371 men spread across six counties. One train alone carried 1,200 to 1,500 men, two Gatling guns, and an artillery battery. He had noticed during the Civil War that an overwhelming concentration of force squelched fighting, which it did again.

That month, according to biographer Olcott, McKinley "watched every movement of the troops for a period of sixteen days, remaining in his office nightly until long after midnight and frequently telegraphing instructions as late as 3 A.M."[10] Miners in some localities adopted resolutions condemning the governor for sending troops, but in their anger they also criticized United Mine Workers President John McBride for advising them against stopping the trains by force.[11]

Conservatives deplored the cost of so large a mobilization. "Bridge burners, trainwreckers and highwaymen are usually shot on sight," opined the Cleveland *Plain Dealer*. The Chicago *Herald* conjoined McKinley's name with that of populist-leaning Illinois Democratic Governor John Altgeld, regretting that both men had appeased "desperadoes and outlaws."[12] Historian Paul Kleppner, in a study of late-nineteenth-century Midwestern politics, found McKinley most concerned for the workers. He found sending troops "something of a traumatic experience. He knew the miners there, had campaigned among them, and had overcome the religious animosity that Catholic and Lutheran miners harbored towards his party. He was cognizant of the impact his use of troops would have. . . . Unlike Altgeld, he did not seek opportunities to deploy his forces; he sought to avoid those opportunities. When they could no longer be avoided, he used the state militia."[13]

The problems of the Hocking Valley miners were not over. By January 1895, in winter and with little money put away, many were destitute, and emissaries approached McKinley, who asked local authorities to convene advisory meetings and report back. Just before midnight on January 9, they telegraphed, "Immediate relief needed." Here is biographer Olcott's description of what happened:

> By five o'clock in the morning a [railroad] car had been loaded with provisions and by nine o'clock it was in Nelsonville, and the work of distribution begun. The governor personally ordered the supplies and agreed to pay for them, but when his friends heard of it they insisted upon bearing their share of the obligation. The governor gave instructions that every appeal was to be met and that nobody should be allowed to go hungry. He wrote to the chambers of commerce of the principal cities and through them made an inquiry into the exact conditions. Finding many families in destitute circumstances, he made a statewide appeal for charity, with the result that he was able to distribute enough money, food, clothing and other necessities to relieve the distress of 2722 miners and their families, representing at least 10,000 persons.[14]

Such was the record of the Ohio governor later caricatured by cartoonists as a puppet of harsh and remote capitalism. The reality was altogether different.

VOX POPULI VOX DEI

McKinley, remarked future Republican House Speaker Joe Cannon, had his ears so close to the ground they filled with grasshoppers. Others simply called him a weak, second-rate man anxious to please everyone and content to let public opinion make up his mind

The correct explanation, readily apparent during McKinley's congressional and gubernatorial tenures, lay in his respect for the American people. But he had also evolved an unusual, even confusing, manner of pursuing politics and policy making. Most politicians who saw McKinley as a follower of public opinion simultaneously recognized his commitment as well as his interpretive mastery. Senator Chauncey Depew said that his "faith in the public intelligence and conscience was supreme. He believed that the people knew more than any man. He never tried to lead but studied so constantly public opinion that he became almost infallible in its interpretation."[15]

More was involved, though, than just shrewd perception. The Ohioan read the newspapers carefully and took every opportunity to ask, "How do people feel about this up your way?" Not just a finger feeling the wind, his inquiries mirrored his preoccupation with the citizenry's role in American democracy. Public opinion and participation, he thought, gave politics life. All of his biographers have emphasized how, as congressman, governor, and president, he insisted upon the public having access to shake his hand, visit his various offices, and otherwise impose on his time. Improving press access to the presidency was a further logical corollary.

As a Republican, McKinley would freely disparage what nineteenth-century politics referred to as "the Democracy"—the political institution of the Democratic party. Democracy with a small *d*, however, was at the core of his politics. In 1900, as president, he offered one audience a rare philosophical explanation: "Your voice, when constitutionally expressed, is commanding and conclusive. It is the law to Congress and the Executive."[16] This conviction explained his behavior, as Mark Hanna captured in a 1901 eulogy: "The one absorbing purpose in William McKinley's political career was to keep closely in touch with the people. . . ."[17]

Where Senator Depew and others erred was about McKinley never trying to lead. In Congress, he did so on labor and trade matters; as president, he would do so in promoting tariff reciprocity and international arbitration, resisting Spanish-American War fever in 1898, and later urging U.S. acquisition of the Philippines. His own war years had been the early crucible of his beliefs, and his White House chief secretary, George Cortelyou, later underscored how

McKinley recollected the fallibility of the public from 1861 to 1865: "the bitter hostility to Stanton and Grant—that Grant was called 'the butcher.'" Public war moods, in particular, were not always to be followed.[18] The civic virtue of the wartime volunteers, on the other hand, had been a particular source of McKinley's democratic faith.

Another chief executive had already made the same point. In July 1861, while Private McKinley was still at Camp Chase, Ohio, President Lincoln had sent Congress a message praising the volunteer army. "There are many single regiments," said Lincoln, "whose members, one and another, possess full practical knowledge of all the arts, sciences, professions and whatever else, whether useful or elegant, is known in the world; and there is scarcely one, from which there could not be selected a President, a Cabinet, a Congress, and perhaps a Court, abundantly competent to administer the government itself."[19]

McKinley's own Twenty-third Ohio Regiment, as we have seen, was one such unit, and its four-year commitment remained a lifetime inspiration. In an 1889 speech, he recalled "the elevated patriotism of the rank and file of the army and their unselfish consecration to the country." Knowing only that the Union was threatened, the men had volunteered in such numbers that "the whole North was turned into a camp for muster and military instruction."[20] This youthful awe, kept alive by many ceremonial visits to the memorials to the Twenty-third Regiment's dead in Poland's Riverside Cemetery and in Cleveland's Woodland Cemetery, helped to explain his deep ongoing commitment to the role and voice of an informed citizenry.

Biographer Morgan summed up this Lincolnesque view of a president's responsibility to the people:

> He was not the people's slave, but their servant. . . . To him, the art of politics was the reconciliation of divergent interests. Government, he thought, functioned for the people, to further the total good. He had few qualms about federal power; he would be alien to subsequent generations of Republicans if they understood him.[21]

Soothing his own generation of Republican officeholders and contributors while he tried to implement a deeply felt broader popular commitment may have been one motivation for keeping his policy positions vague and cloaked in homilies.

A SKEPTIC OF THE CORPORATIONS?

As a congressman and governor, McKinley discussed corporations in speeches, although rarely by that name. He never made a major address or statement seeking to define a corporate role in politics and society.

Setting out clear and specific views might have been unwise. As a powerful friend of enterprise, industry, and tariff protection, McKinley was well regarded by business leaders. Their approval presumably was reenforced by opposition newspaper portraiture of the Ohioan as a compliant supporter of the tariff magnates and the men with the diamond stickpins. Years before, Mark Hanna had taken away a contrary first impression: the nature of McKinley's 1876 legal defense of strikers (employed by Hanna's family coal company). Management practices, insisted the young lawyer, were at least as much to blame for the violence.

During his early years in Congress, he frequently introduced petitions on behalf of Grange organizations supporting railroad regulation. He also helped Grange-backed Republicans in state and local elections and spoke for regulatory provisions in the Interstate Commerce Act of 1887 and elsewhere. We have seen his attention to arbitration, unusual in an era when many businessmen preferred the cheaper alternatives of Pinkerton agents and bayonets. Tariff legislation he mostly applauded for keeping American wages far above Europe's. His remarks in Congress were often accompanied by wage charts. "It is labor I would protect," he said.[22]

Corporations per se seem to have had less appeal. Although he took election support from Republican coffers largely filled with business contributions, he showed no interest in accepting the jobs, fees, and directorships proferred during decades when there was no legal constraint. His early biographer Charles Olcott noted that despite the demands on his congressional pay from his wife's medical and nursing expenses, McKinley declined a ten-thousand-dollar engagement to give ten lectures on protectionism, as well as an offer to become the attorney for a large Western railroad at twenty-five thousand dollars a year.[23] As governor, he turned down an invitation to join the board of directors of a major New York life insurance firm, which paid eight thousand dollars a year for attending only one meeting a year.[24]

One biographer noted that McKinley as a congressman "often publicly condemned" what he described in one talk as the "mad spirit for gain and riches which is so prevalent in American society . . . by gambling in stock, speculation in wheat, by 'corners' and 'margins.'"[25] He himself shunned these things. He stayed in Congress because his commitment was to the processes of government—not every regime, but the purposeful "Government" of the North and of Lincoln. In one paragraph in his wartime journal, *government* was the only word he began with a capital letter.[26]

Congressman McKinley did not have a lot to say about the trusts. In 1888, he was critical, saying, "I have no sympathy with combinations, organized for this or any purpose, to control the supply and therefore control prices," and he praised the enactment of the Sherman Antitrust Act in 1890 for striking at "trusts or unlawful combinations of capital to raise prices according to their own sweet will, and extort undue profits from the mass of the people."[27] He thereupon cooled his rhetoric, presumably awaiting action. However, the authority of the Sherman Act sparked few prosecutions either by Republican Benjamin Harrison in 1891 and 1892 or by Democrat Grover Cleveland during the 1893–96 period. A crippling ruling by the Supreme Court in *The United States* v. *E. C. Knight Co.* put the effectiveness of congressional antitrust regulation under a legal cloud in both the 1896 and the 1900 political debates.

Even so, the omnipresence of corporate money and influence in Gilded Age politics has obliged the most favorable historians to ponder McKinley's rationalizations: "Some private legerdemain must have reconciled him to the 'practical' methods that were employed. . . . He scrupulously shunned the bribe and the bargain, but his purity must have involved an intricate self-deception, a timely looking away and convenient forgetfulness."[28]

There was an obvious precedent. Alexander Hamilton, whom McKinley had admired, also tolerated speculation and corruption, even in people close to him, to promote causes he cherished: the late-eighteenth-century launching of the Bank of the United States and the federal assumption and funding of state Revolutionary War debt. Hamilton's self-exculpation was that corruption is inevitable and that he himself satisfied honor by not profiting personally. McKinley had a similar commitment to the protective system and likewise declined to profit. He would not invest in any business affected by the tariff, in one instance returning five thousand dollars worth of stock in cotton mills set aside for him by a friend.[29]

As governor, his early efforts were more against than for corporations. He pursued steps to regulate railroads and assure coal mine safety. Corporations were peeved by his quiet success in getting the Ohio legislature to establish $1,000 fines and six-month jail sentences for employers who refused to permit employees to join unions, a statutory rarity in the business-dominated 1890s.[30]

In another departure from typical Republican thinking, McKinley, shortly after his inauguration as governor, moved against the Ohio tax laws that heavily burdened home owners yet barely taxed investments. He appointed an expert commission, which in 1893 reported back with a recommendation for levies on corporations, franchises, and intangible wealth. By one assessment, although McKinley kept harping on the need for tax reform, he was overtly neutral and never referred to corporations "except by implication."[31]

Another biographer perceived tactical ingenuousness: "McKinley deftly stood above the strife, though all concerned knew that his sympathies lay against the corporations. Again, he refused to use the issue for partisan purposes, wisely seeing that that would crystallize opposition to the new program if he did. He remained silent, using private pressure to enact laws while making no enemies and losing no support. The laws finally passed during his second [state] administration taxed railroads, foreign corporations doing business in Ohio, and telegraph, telephone and express operators."[32]

His earlier votes in Congress for the Interstate Commerce Act of 1887 and the Sherman Antitrust Act were less revealing. Both measures were part political facade and were broadly supported in consequence. McKinley's priorities as governor, where his leader-ship could produce law, tell us more.

As to his deeper motivation, one can only speculate. By the late 1880s and early 1890s, many old Lincolnians still active in politics and government were gnashing their teeth at the rise of great corpo-rations and an attendant plutocracy. Among them was McKinley's great patron, Rutherford Hayes. The ex-president, always some-thing of a father figure to Congressman McKinley, would preside at his protégé's 1892 swearing-in as governor, only a year before Hayes's own death in 1893.

Hayes's doubts about corporate capitalism antedated his White House tenure. Like McKinley in Congress, Hayes as Ohio's governor in the 1870s had favored the Granger agenda of state railroad regula-tion. In an 1871 speech, he voiced larger doubts about "the colossal fortunes which, under the sanction of law, are already consolidating into the hands of a few men." At that point, he merely urged a response from "the home, the school, the platform, the pulpit and the press" and shrank from corrective action by government.[33]

In 1877, newly inaugurated as president, Hayes acceded to a request by the governors of West Virginia, Maryland, Pennsylvania, and Illinois to send federal troops to curb violence in that year's great railroad strikes. In discussions with his cabinet, however, he "raised the point then that if railroad workers were to be subjected to governmental force, perhaps the railroads should be subjected to governmental supervision in their labor policies."[34] On August 4, 1877, he wrote in his diary that perhaps the real remedy was "judi-cious control of the capitalists."[35]

Out of the White House, after 1881, Hayes grew angrier. In 1886, he told a Toledo audience that "government cannot long endure if property is largely in a few hands and large masses of people are unable to earn homes, education and support in old age." Two years later, he favored blocking "a permanent aristocracy of wealth" by legislation that would limit inheritance to five hundred thou-sand dollars, the rest to go to the state.[36] Hayes's campaign biogra-pher back in 1876, a young Ohioan, William Dean Howells, found fame by the late eighties as a novelist attacking the disparities that so aroused Hayes. The ex-president, taking a cue from Howells's writing, wondered in his diary if he, Hayes, wasn't becoming a nihilist:

> I use it to mean all opinions tending to show the wrong and evils of the money-piling tendency of our country, which is changing laws, government and morals and giving all powers to the rich and bringing in pauperism and its attendant crimes and wretchedness like a flood. Lincoln was for a government of the people. The new tendency is "a government of the rich, by the rich and for the rich." The man who sees this and is opposed to it, I call a "nihilist."[37]

Had the ex-president ever used the term *nihilist* in talking with William McKinley, the latter would have dismissed it as an irrelevant foreignism. Hayes had gone to Harvard Law School, while McKinley had spent his college-age years in Colonel-Professor Hayes's school of wartime commitment and practical patriotism. The younger, more practical man knew that Hayes's open reformism was part of what had crippled his presidency. At the same time, given their closeness, McKinley must have heard and respected Hayes's views. When his former colonel died, McKinley led the eulogies, singling out his social concern and good works as well as his patriotism.

Indeed, the two families were close enough to have shared their White Houses over the decades. In 1877, the new Congressman McKinley and his wife spent two weeks residing in the White House to keep an eye on the younger Hayes children when their parents were away. Around that time, Mrs. Hayes's niece married McKinley's best friend. In 1901, the eldest son, Webb Hayes, was one of the few nonfamily members to be present during the last hours when McKinley died of his bullet wounds.

Hayes had served Ohio as congressman and governor, and when McKinley followed in both offices, his priorities—tariffs, a mild Granger view of railroad regulation, attention to coal mine safety, deep concern that troops sent in to deal with labor violence should respect the rights of the strikers—were much like those of his mentor. On taking the governor's office in 1892, one of McKinley's first acts was to hang a life-sized portrait of Rutherford Hayes. There is no direct proof, but the views of corporations and capitalist excesses voiced by Hayes and other old Lincoln men probably influenced the late-nineteenth-century worldview that McKinley so carefully refrained from setting out in both Columbus and Washington.

MCKINLEY'S FOCAL POINT: THE TARIFF

McKinley's enthusiasm for protective tariffs was part of what led foes to call him a front man for corporations, trusts, and plutocrats. Friends, by contrast, tied his tariff support to high wages for labor and commitment to a system that nurtured U.S. industry and inventiveness.

His intentions, at least, seem to have been lofty. When he came to Congress, the Ohioan's goal was a new version of the old "American System" of Henry Clay built around tariff rates keyed to "the greatest good for the greatest number." In later years, his speeches displayed an almost encyclopedic knowledge of wage levels in U.S. industries versus those of their foreign competitors. The weakness in his Ohio-centered view, though, was that while it supported his almost religious commitment to protection, by the 1880s and 1890s, it kept him from appreciating several growing side effects of high tariffs—sustenance for not a few monopolies and trusts, as well as grab-bag profits for industries with well-placed senators, congressmen, or lobbyists on their side.

In the Washington of the 1880s, tariff making involved lobbyists and organized interest groups running amok. As McKinley rose in influence, he came to hate the work of lobbyists in parochializing and all but mocking his "greatest good" calculus. However, as Republican House floor leader and chairman of the Ways and Means Committee from 1889 to 1891, he could not criticize the processes involved, at least publicly, without losing his own very influential insider's baton. The result, in 1890, was his name on the famous McKinley Tariff, despite his private understanding of its excesses.

"No tariff bill was ever framed that was not largely made up by compromises," McKinley admitted. During the 1880s, the stakes and interest-group pressures—tariff legislation always began in the House, changed markedly in the Senate, and then emerged in overloaded form from a conference committee—intensified with the successes and demands of U.S. industrialization. By 1890, McKinley himself became a procedural victim. "Many of the changes I do not like, but you see there is no time to specify," he said of the bill as reported from the Senate. "I scarcely know what will be the end of it."[38]

Later, as president, he confided to a member of his cabinet: "You misapprehend my attitude as to the protective tariff. I was chairman of the committee in the House which advocated the tariff rates under a bill known as the McKinley bill, but I thought then, and think now [1897], that it is for our best interests to return gradually to a much less drastic system of tariff." Asked why he accepted the high rates of 1890, he said, "For the best reason in the world, to get my bill passed. My idea was to get the act through Congress, and to make necessary reductions later."[39]

A half century before, in the early stages of the tariff debate, things had been simpler. Voters faced three broad and seemingly distinctive options. The first, a revenue tariff, did not seek to protect U.S. industries. It raised funds, solely for revenue needs, by charges on imports like tea, coffee, sugar, silk, cocoa, and wine. Choice number two, pure free trade, levied few duties, raised little money, and had little support. The third, a protective system, set tariffs around schedules designed to let U.S. industries reach adulthood without being overwhelmed by the cheaper products of advanced manufacturing nations like Britain. Most other nations also employed protection in varying forms and degrees.

In the United States of the mid-nineteenth century, farmers, importers, merchants, shippers, and a considerable number of bankers favored a revenue tariff only. So did manufacturers who imported raw materials. The Democratic tariffs implemented in the 1840s and 1850s emphasized revenue, with only a mild component of protection. Then, during the Civil War, the North under Abraham Lincoln and the Republicans embraced full-scale protectionism, which provided large revenues and nurtured some war-related industries. Between 1859 and 1889, the source of value added in the U.S. economy shifted from almost two-to-one dominance for agriculture to a 47 percent to 35 percent margin for industry.

By 1890, the very success of that transformation suggested some reshaping. Britain's own metamorphosis from farm to factory between 1800 and 1830 had also spurred new thinking. As industry matured, attention in parliament swung from protection's economic armor to mechanisms for export promotion. In consequence, the centuries-old system ranging from the Navigation Acts (upholding British shipping and commerce) to tariffs, subsidies, and the laws prohibiting the emigration of skilled industrial workers was phased out between the 1820s and 1840s.

By 1890, McKinley was among those realizing the need to modify the U.S. system. In this vein, while developing industries still needed help, Washington policy makers also talked of reforming customs procedures, improving rate-setting practices (to make adjudication more scientific and less an interest-group melee), reducing high rates that needlessly sheltered trusts and monopolies, and replacing inflexible schedules with reciprocity provisions that could be used to promote exports. Coming to Congress in 1877, McKinley knew Ohio products like iron, steel, and wool, although as economic grounding, he had only the practical but narrow touch of his wartime regimental quartermaster experience and some knowledge of commercial law.

Yet he proved a surprisingly fast learner. By 1881, the third-term congressman was applauding President Chester Arthur's proposal to set up a federal tariff commission to adjust the rate schedule on a more progressive and scientific basis. In 1884, McKinley helped put such a plank in the national Republican platform.[40] In 1890, as chairman of the House Ways and Means Committee, he drafted the legislation sought by the Harrison administration to improve the customs service and root out abuses and corruption in the overall administration of customs collection.[41]

The 1890 McKinley Tariff Act, even after its gross overloading in the Senate and in conference, included a reciprocity provision conceived by James G. Blaine but pushed by McKinley. This provision, while allowing Latin American goods liberal access, gave the president leverage to impose duties to penalize such products if those nations did not give free entry to certain U.S. goods in return.[42] It counted a number of successes. The 1890 act also set up a mechanism for rebating tariffs paid on raw materials by manufacturers who made those materials into goods for export. The Democrats scotched the reciprocity provision in their 1894 tariff but, as president, McKinley brought it back in 1897, which is a subject for chapter 5.

The supremely innovative State of Ohio that McKinley upheld was no fiction, witness Firestone, Hall, Goodrich, Brush, Studebaker, Packard, and the rest. Yet in many other states, accumulating evidence showed how trusts and monopolies fattened on tariff favoritism. Ohioans could counter that two trusts locally familiar—oil and whiskey—owed nothing to import restraints. John D. Rockefeller had gotten started in northeast Ohio with no tariff help, and in the early nineteenth century, the southern part of the state, like adjacent Pennsylvania and Kentucky, had been a center of U.S. whiskey making. But these were something of an anomaly.

If McKinley for too long dismissed the real connections between some protective tariff rates and monopoly formation, his Stark County domicile also blinded him to a second linkage: between tariffs and great wealth accumulations. It was not that way in Canton, which hummed with protected industries while the owners lived unostentatiously. Even in the late 1930s, the *Ohio (State) Guide* offered this description of its best residential district: "tidy streets packed with the rather modest homes of Canton's wealthier citizens. There is no large class distinction in the city: even the most affluent residents do not make a special display of wealth."[43]

The labor genesis of McKinley's tariff commitment had its own blinders. To historian Morgan, "his precarious political district, his personal background of self-made success all committed him to further the cause of labor. He supported immigration to help labor; he believed in protection largely because it insured prosperity for the worker; he favored some form of monetary inflation because he believed that it helped the masses; and he favored regulating corporate influence in government because he feared that it boded ill for balanced national development if one interest outstripped the others."[44] By the early nineties, despite high industry wage levels, the excesses taking over the tariff system generally added to the imbalance in favor of corporations.

Between early 1892, when McKinley took over Ohio's governorship, and January 1896, when he left Columbus to return to

Canton as the front-runner for that year's Republican presidential nomination, the imbalance had become a national discussion. Wealth concentration had become obscene. The agrarian West and South were in economic revolt, and the currency and tariff systems were conjoined as culprits. Most future Progressives, from TR and La Follette to Woodrow Wilson, joined McKinley in spurning the Populist agenda because of its radicalism. But McKinley himself was also suspect in some fashionable circles.

MUGWUMPS AND MISPERCEPTIONS

In 1884, several dozen prominent upper-middle-class Republicans and independents who supported Democrat Grover Cleveland's presidential candidacy got themselves a name that history has remembered and in many quarters even gilded: mugwumps. More than most of their contemporaries, these men—there were no notable female mugwumps—seem to have captured the label of reform, which helps explain why McKinley's politics and domestic policies did not.

Centered in major cities like Boston, New York, Chicago, and St. Louis, and at leading universities, the mugwumps by and large shared a lengthy list of commitments: strong opposition to protective tariffs, enthusiasm for civil service reform, distaste for silver and monetary inflation (they insisted on the gold standard), hostility to railroad regulation, strikes, and labor unions, skepticism of excessive democracy, and disdain for the political rule of state and local bosses, grubby Republican small businessmen, or Tammany chieftains alike. Yale Professor William Graham Sumner, best known for lauding free trade and invoking survival of the fittest, also captured the prevailing mugwump cultural hauteur: "I am unable to see how a boyhood spent in poverty among simple people peculiarly qualifies a man for political preferment, but such seems to be the general argument. . . ."[45]

Not a few of the mugwumps had earlier spurned Grant for Horace Greeley and the Liberal Republican movement in 1872; their last cause was to reject McKinley in 1900 by rallying anti-imperialist opposition to U.S. policy in the Philippines. So when Americans think of political as opposed to economic reform in the years from Grant down to McKinley, mugwump names leap out of friendly history books. They include George W. Curtis, E. L. Godkin, Charles Francis Adams, Henry Adams, Brooks Adams, Charles Eliot, Edward Atkinson, David Wells, Horace White, Charles Eliot Norton, Thomas Wentworth Higginson, William Graham Sumner, and others.

Mostly educators, editors, or authors, they were well connected. Their prevailing mind-set was professional class, unsympathetic to free silverites, southern and eastern European immigrants, labor unions, agrarian radicals, or tobacco-chewing industrial Republicans from the Midwest. Their rapport was with the antiprotectionist mercantile, legal, banking, and shipping elites of the major coastal cities, especially Boston and New York. A survey of New York mugwumps who endorsed Cleveland in 1884 found that out of a sample of 396, a quarter could be found in the *Social Register*.[46]

There was little of this about McKinley, even though he partially agreed with their views on political bossism and civil service reform (and shared the Civil War–era abolitionism of some). In addition to his Ohio labor, Granger, silver bimetallist, and churchgoing Methodist sentiments, he had another unappreciated sentiment: interest in securing and expanding voting rights, for both blacks and women.

Ida McKinley's family, the Saxtons, believed in women's rights. Before marrying, she had become a teller at the family bank in Canton, despite her youth sometimes taking over in her father's absence. In a local debate around the time of their marriage, William McKinley took the side of voting rights for women. In 1872, when the Equal Rights party nominated Ohio-born Victoria Woodhull for president, he hosted her in Canton.

McKinley, alone among nineteenth-century presidents, received an honorary doctorate from two women's colleges, Smith and Mount Holyoke in Massachusetts. In Virginia, he made a special visit to Randolph-Macon Women's College, founded by the Methodists in 1893. Although just four Western states, Colorado, Idaho, Utah, and Wyoming, gave women the vote at the time, McKinley told the Holyoke students, "I am glad that we are demonstrating in the United States today that the boy should have no more advantage than the girl."[47]

By contrast, Grover Cleveland had observed that "the relative positions of men and women were assigned long ago by a higher intelligence."[48] The mugwumps, more interested in narrowing the franchise, opposed expanding it to include women.

Cleveland, with a party base in the South, supported white rule there, whereas McKinley's youthful abolitionism still guided him to support black voting rights during the Cleveland years. As we will see, during his own presidency, McKinley continued to take an interest, albeit a flagging one, in black federal appointments and opportunities for military service. The Republican party was giving in to popular opinion and the insistence of the white Democratic South on disenfranchising all but a small portion of its black voters.

Had McKinley been more of a mugwump and less of a "small *d*" democrat, he might have fared better with the arbiters of reform in the 1890s and later decades. But his views did not fit. Besides his unfashionable taste for labor, Midwest Methodism, and the Grange, McKinley was also amenable to sitting within range of a cuspidor with fellow tobacco-chewing congressmen who didn't know Hawthorne the poet from hawthorn the tree. Worse still, in mugwump eyes, he occasionally indulged his own distaste for effete Easterners. The only supporters of across-the-board tariff cuts, McKinley once told the House, were feather-brained reformers and men with private incomes, adding to chuckles that "that class of gentlemen 'neither reap nor sow, and do not gather into barns.' "[49] He had more faith, he said, in puddlers and potters than in the university departments, so strongly influenced by English economic fashion, that ignored wage levels and taught free trade.

By many definitions, McKinley was a democrat and an egalitarian, and, by some, a reformer. However, he was certainly no reformer by the yardsticks of fashionable mugwumpery, and their dismissals have added to the confusion of his ideological memory and political legacy, clouding his achievement.

BUCKEYE BIMETALLISM

Free coinage of silver became a credo of cranks after the 1896 Bryan campaign. Gold turned into a "barbarous relic" after the United States abandoned the gold standard in 1933. Neither metal, then, has enjoyed the subsequent verdict of history. Yet in the quarter century after 1873, no American political issue throbbed more deeply.

Through 1878, moreover, silver was a serious cause even to many who later recanted. After the Civil War's end, the federal government let the currency contract from its swollen, inflationary wartime levels. This shrinkage took place despite the large population increase between 1865 and 1875 from North-South reunification and renewed heavy European immigration. The stock market panic of 1873 led into a major economic downturn, which further aggravated the contraction. The upshot was that the per capita money supply fell from $30.35 in 1865 to $25.72 in 1866, ten years later bottoming at a painfully deflationary $17.51.[50] This brought hard times. George Armstrong Custer's cavalry command wasn't the only enterprise wiped out in 1876; many farmers and businessmen felt scarcely better off.

In the iron and steel industry, producers who had borrowed to expand gloomed as the price of a long ton of pig iron dropped from $49 in 1872 to $30 in 1874 and $18 in 1878 before rebounding to $29 in 1880. Pennsylvania and Ohio, the American seat of Vulcan, also represented a monetary transition zone where Eastern financial support for a gold standard gave way to Midwestern and Western demand for a currency expansion friendly to borrowers and continued fast growth. In the 1870s, this meant enthusiasm for greenbacks (the Civil War currency with no metallic backing), silver, or any plausible vehicle of monetary expansion. Peter Cooper, the minor Greenback party presidential nominee in 1876, was no rube but a millionaire pillar of the U.S. iron industry.

Down through the centuries, at least across the developed world, silver and gold had shared a role in most nations' money, usually keeping much the same ratio of respective value. In the 1870s, however, that longtime fifteen- or sixteen-to-one relationship between an ounce of gold and a much cheaper ounce of silver broke down. New discoveries and technologies were responsible. After California's Gold Rush, the yellow metal became more plentiful; that made silver gain relative value. As the 1870s began, however, scarcity dynamics looked about to change: mining experts anticipated a flood of silver, which would reduce that metal's relative value and purchasing power.

Chronology is pivotal in assessing the gold-silver equation. In 1870, Britain was the only major nation on a gold monometallic standard; the German states had silver coins; China and India used silver; the United States and France were bimetallic under law, if not always in practice. Silver was no political cause in the United States of the late 1860s; its price was high enough that silver dollars, if minted, would just be melted down. In 1873, however, with the United States sliding into what would be a deep five-year economic downturn and the per capita money supply shrinking, the silver mines of the American West began producing ever larger quantities of the white metal.

This pushed the greenback issue into the shade, although the Greenback party continued to run presidential candidates in 1880 and 1884. Practically speaking, between the mid-1870s and 1878, those who wanted to help farmers or businessmen suffering from low prices and high debt turned to silver. The question about putting some more silver into the U.S. money supply was not whether but how much. Renewed coinage of silver dollars was widely agreed to. The more ambitious wanted to resume full coinage and convertibility of silver at the familiar gold-to-silver ratio of sixteen to one.

But while this wasn't radical historically, what started to make it so by the late seventies was so great a silver production in Nevada, Montana, and Colorado that the old sixteen-to-one ratio buckled. In gold terms, the value of the silver in a minted dollar dropped from $1.00 in 1873 to 99 cents in 1874, 96 in 1875, 89 in 1876, and 92 in 1877.[51] Think of this as an inverse fever chart: at 98.6 on the thermometer—a silver dollar being worth 98.6 cents in gold— free coinage of silver at the old ratio would have worked. However, as the value of silver in gold terms dropped, the feverish aspect rose. Free and unlimited sixteen-to-one coinage with silver worth just 85 or 88 in gold clearly would cause inflation. And by Gresham's law, cheap silver currency would drive out gold coins.

McKinley had entered the halls of Congress in 1877, hailing from an Ohio district where the wheatfields shaded into iron and coal country. The Ohio legislature, hectored by farmers and iron makers alike, had just passed a resolution calling on Congress to reintroduce silver dollars. McKinley, in company with most other Ohio Republican congressmen in 1878, backed the proposal for free silver coinage at sixteen-to-one sponsored by Missouri Representative Richard "Silver Dick" Bland. The Republican Senate balked, and the bipartisan compromise worked out that year, named the Bland-Allison Act, authorized only limited government purchase and coinage of silver. Full-scale, unlimited coinage could have been a monetary disaster, given that between 1870 and 1890, U.S. silver production quadrupled.[52]

By the 1890s, free coinage was a "solution" born only of the genuine desperation of the Plains wheat belt and the self-interest of Rocky Mountain silver interests in raising the price of a market-glutting commodity. In the mid-1870s, with the glut only beginning and the metal in a silver dollar worth ninety-odd cents, one could argue that U.S. government buying of silver for large-scale coinage might have turned the valuation tide. Instead, as the U.S. government began accumulating gold in 1877 in order to resume full gold convertibility by 1879, gold prices rose and silver prices fell further.

As one measure of its mid-1870s respectability, the case for silver adoption at that time was made ninety years later by America's leading monetary historian (and political conservative) Milton Friedman. His argument was that embracing silver would have expanded the money supply and avoided the evil of sharp deflation: "The adoption of silver instead of gold by the U.S. in 1879 might well have largely eliminated the decline that actually occurred in the gold price of silver and have permitted roughly stable prices in both gold and silver countries."[53]

McKinley, like most Ohio Republicans, tended during the eighties to favor only whatever silver relief was compatible with "sound money." Like most others, he coupled his support for resumption of the gold standard with backing for periodic prosilver legislation like the Sherman Silver Purchase Act of 1890. Urged by the Republican Harrison administration, this measure committed the government to a recalculated level of silver purchases. John Sherman, in 1890 the U.S. Treasury secretary for whom the Silver Purchase Act was named, was a favorite son of the Ohio GOP.

In contrast to the gold-oriented East, Ohio had a mild taste for easy money and debtor relief going right back to the early days after the Civil War. The "Ohio Idea" of 1868, promoted by Buckeye Democratic Congressman George S. Pendleton, proposed that the U.S. Treasury pay off the principal on federal government bonds in greenbacks rather than gold. During the 1870s, Ohioans in the iron and steel business, including Clevelander Mark Hanna, shared in the silver sentiment. Fifteen years later, one of them, Adiram Warner, a Marietta coal and iron dealer and former Union Civil War general, would head the American Bimetallic League, which became a national force in the 1890s. Jacob Coxey, who led "Coxey's Army" of the unemployed from Ohio to Washington in 1894, came from Massillon, just a few miles from Canton. His scoffed-at demand was to give the unemployed jobs building good roads, the costs to be paid by legal tender (neither gold- nor silver-backed) issued by the U.S. Treasury.

The Ohio GOP posture—counted quite responsible in Cleveland and Cincinnati—was to support gold in a framework of bimetallism. U.S. House Speaker Thomas Brackett Reed of Maine, McKinley's ineffectual rival for the 1896 GOP presidential nomination, fairly remarked that as between the gold bugs and the silver bugs, McKinley was a "straddle bug." Most Ohioans were. By 1890, as chairman of the House Ways and Means Committee, he had evolved a relatively sophisticated position: a reasonable amount of silver coinage would be a good thing to fight deflation and off-and-on currency contraction. Free coinage at sixteen-to-one, however, would be disastrous. Given silver's low value at that date, convertibility would drain the U.S. gold supply and put the nation on a de facto silver standard. That, in turn, would cripple rapidly expanding U.S. international commerce. For bimetallism to be workable, said McKinley, would require an international conference, with British concurrence in drawing up binding guidelines.

This was not the preferred position of the banking and commercial East, to whom gold was economic religion. However, Republican national platforms straddled to cater to the Midwest and West—and in 1896, as chapter 5 will pursue, McKinley's own platform, guided by himself and Mark Hanna, evolved through straddle-bug nuances to a final-hour bimetallic-hedged gold commitment that Niccolò Machiavelli himself would have found suitably Florentine in its timing and effect.

The William McKinley who sought and won the Republican nomination in 1896 was no Eastern Wall Street backer or apologist for the burgeoning trusts. He was too much of a Middle West democrat and Lincolnian. That was part of why he enjoyed so much popularity among Americans and rank-and-file Republicans alike.

Part II

Becoming and Being President

3

McKinley and the
Realignment of 1896

The years from 1893 to 1896 witnessed the first major voting realignment in American politics since the 1850s. . . . William Jennings
Bryan, as a political spokesman for evangelical Protestants, drew a
number of Protestant Republican voters into the Democratic Party,
while William McKinley established strong new roots among many
urban-industrial immigrant and labor voters.

Samuel P. Hays, *The American Party Systems*

Much of McKinley's success in the presidency came from the rare
strength and sophistication he showed in winning it. This is central
to any understanding of the man and what he achieved, albeit
behind his mask of conventional thinking.

The election of 1896 was a multiple breakthrough. It marked
the first time since Lincoln's day that a nationally well-known and
powerful Republican politician won his party's presidential nomination on the first ballot—and did so by beating, rather than sub-
mitting to, the Eastern machine forces. Lincoln himself, in 1860,
took until the third ballot to edge past Senator William H. Seward,
New York's choice.

For the first time since Northern occupation forces left the
South two decades earlier, the Grand Old Party of 1896 put
together a national majority. Indeed, McKinley's triumph marked
the Republicans' first popular majority in a reassembled, demilita-
rized nation. Urban, industrial America—the new nation of tele-
phones, turbines, and bustling immigrant sidewalks—now had a
political cycle.

But was it *his* milestone, a McKinley realignment and cycle? The interpretations are almost polar. The prevailing mid-twentieth-century view, seeded by the 1896–98 political attacks of the Hearst and Pulitzer newspapers, casts McKinley as a mediocrity, a pleasant, amiable man of no great merit who just happened to be the party choice in the year when scared businessmen and financiers led by Mark Hanna raised the record millions needed to turn back the Bryan challenge. By this argument, they, not McKinley, implanted a new long generation of supremacy for steel mill and railroad car Republicanism.

A second, newer school credits the personal architecture of McKinley, a clever and strong-minded Ohio politician, helped by Mark Hanna, who almost worshiped him. After capturing the nomination against determined machine opposition, he went on to win an 1896 general election victory no other Republican could have brought about. This, more or less, is the view of his late-twentieth-century biographers.

Not that any such achievement is cemented by a single election. McKinley's judgments and luck consolidated a new GOP era during his five years as president. Republican successes in midterm elections of 1898 and 1902 ended a quarter-century pattern of administrations usually being politically crippled at midpoint. The selection of Theodore Roosevelt as McKinley's running mate in the triumphant reelection of 1900—decided over Hanna's objection—worked to extend the GOP consolidation for seven additional years after McKinley's assassination.

The Hearst-Pulitzer interpretation is mostly calumny grown stale. Not only does McKinley deserve the stature of a realignment president, but the personal-to-his-own-candidacy dimension of the electoral victory underpins the scope of his overall achievement. He was also a hinge president in governmental innovation and in domestic and foreign policy.

THE MAKING OF THE PRESIDENT, 1876–96

Had some post–Civil War chronicler achieved what Theodore White did with his series *The Making of the President 1960, 1964, 1968,* and *1972,* the postbellum sagas of McKinley's Ohio-born predecessors would have split into two streams—the machine captive and the less-than-effectives. Two-term winner Grant, nominated and elected as *the* Northern war hero, was generally controlled in office sometimes simply manipulated—by the Republican party's stalwart faction. Lacking political experience, the great general of Vicksburg, Chattanooga, and the siege of Richmond did not have the substantive and tactical wherewithal to assert himself in the corridors of Washington.

The three next Ohio-born chief executives did rise through politics—Hayes (elected in 1876), Garfield (1880), and Harrison (1888). However, all were compromise nominees decided upon in late convention ballots—the seventh for Hayes, thirty-sixth for Garfield, and eighth for Harrison. Each of their nominations was bestowed by power brokers breaking a stalemate. Even after taking office, each man lacked the personal and political stature to be a dominating chief executive. As a different lesson, John Sherman, Ohio's perennial presidential favorite son, figured in three nomination struggles without ever winning one. A clue lay in his nickname: the Ohio Icicle.

In chronicling McKinley, however, a nineteenth-century Theodore White could have found some quietly impressive drama in the man's steady climb up five mutually supportive ladders: 1) ever-greater prominence in the Ohio Republican party; 2) emergence as the national GOP's principal spokesman on tariff issues; 3) ascent to leadership among Republicans in the House of Representatives; 4) mounting power and visibility at Republican presidential nominating conventions; and 5) achievement of unusual popularity among the national Republican rank and file. In consequence, when McKinley won the White House, it was *his* presidency, even if part of his modus operandi was to disguise that prowess by appearing amenable, collaborative, open to persuasion, and willing to let others take the credit for achieving what was often his own objective all along.

As a newly fledged lawyer, he had spent the eight years of the Grant administration in Canton. But even from afar, McKinley would have perceived Grant's captivity. Hayes he knew especially well, and Garfield enough; he would have taken note of the weaknesses inherent first in their nominations and then in their standing on Capitol Hill. Harrison, a decade later, was crippled by his own prickliness, as well as by the barely hidden disdain of party power brokers. "A stranger to the art of popularizing himself," he was said to make enemies with a personal handshake.[1] Congress—the Senate, in particular—had gained such ascendancy in Washington that by 1885, Woodrow Wilson, a young political scientist at Johns Hopkins, published a book entitled *Congressional Government*. Presidents were subordinate, as the rebukes to Grover Cleveland further confirmed. All this McKinley would have duly noted.

His Ohio origins and connections probably put the presidency in his mind soon after he arrived in Washington. That interest must have turned serious by 1885, and once Harrison got nominated and elected in 1888, opportunity beckoned unmistakably. James G. Blaine and Sherman were old—sixty-three and sixty-nine—and falling by the wayside. Some saw McKinley as the potential national legatee of both. In 1892, Ohio's new favorite son would be forty-nine, in 1896 just fifty-three. It is important to consider his five ladders—in the Ohio GOP, in the U.S. House, in tariff preeminence, in a burgeoning national popularity, and in the high councils of quadrennial Republican presidential nominating—and how they steadily bore him toward higher office. His climb was methodical verging on relentless.

His first two congressional terms (1877–81) thrived on his Ohio connections. Closeness to President Hayes broadened his education, even if it didn't help much in a House of Representatives controlled by the Democrats. McKinley's iron and steel background and knowledgability on tariff matters counted more, getting him picked in 1881 for the Ohio GOP seat on the House Ways and Means Committee. Protectionist House leaders of both parties—Democratic Ways and Means Chairman Samuel Randall of Pennsylvania, Republican Speaker Warren Kiefer of Ohio, and GOP Ways and Means Chairman William "Pig Iron" Kelley of Pennsylvania—all aided his early advance.

In home-state and national GOP conventions, McKinley was a relative neophyte, but a fast-rising one. In 1880, he was named temporary chair and keynoter of the Ohio state convention. Although not selected as a delegate to that year's national convention, he was chosen to serve for a while as Ohio's representative on the Republican National Committee.

Over the next six years, he came of age in both Ohio and Washington. At the off-year Buckeye Republican conventions, where state tickets were negotiated, McKinley usually chaired the resolutions committee. His role in supervising and presenting the platform helped to build his reputation for expertise, conciliation, and highly effective oratory. In 1884, a presidential year, he chaired Ohio's GOP convention. This time, he was also selected as one of the four at-large delegates to the national convention.

At the national party gathering, too, his skills got him named to chair the high-profile resolutions committee—and enjoy unexpected attention. When the convention chairman could not quiet a noisy, unruly floor of delegates, he turned to McKinley, whose commanding voice quickly silenced the hall. Over several days, the Ohio congressman also led a highly visible floor maneuver that helped clear the way for Blaine's nomination.

On Capitol Hill, McKinley was second only to Ways and Means Chairman Kelley as the House GOP tariff spokesman. In Ohio, his prestige now made him chair of the 1885 state convention that nominated the fervid Joseph B. "Fire Alarm Joe" Foraker for governor. After Foraker won, he and Senator John Sherman and McKinley were generally recognized as the three prime movers of state GOP politics.

In 1887, at age forty-four, McKinley began the four critical years that would position him for a presidential bid. No documents, no diaries, no confidential letters to Mark Hanna (or anyone else) contain his secret hopes or veiled stratagems. No memoranda set out the predicaments of the previous Ohio-born presidents or revealed how he planned to do better. Still, for whatever reasons and ambitions, "Major" McKinley—the title he still preferred—carefully set in place the career joists, beams, and buttresses that Grant, Hayes, Garfield, Sherman, and Harrison had each lacked. His sophistication in the nominating processes of the Ohio and national Republican parties dovetailed with wide personal popularity, proven oratory, and, not least, shrewd leadership on the issues complex he expected to dominate the late nineteenth century economic landscape: the protective tariff system and U.S. industrial growth and high-wage employment.

Democratic President Cleveland, in a late 1887 message to Congress, abandoned his New York–based straddling position on tariffs and threw down the glove. Angry that Capitol Hill Republicans had blocked Democratic tariff reductions, he attacked the high protective tariff as a "vicious, inequitable and illogical source of unnecessary taxation." The revenue it raised was "needlessly withdrawn from trade and the people's use."[2] The Democratic platform of 1888 added a further indictment: that high tariffs "permitted and fostered . . . trusts and combinations."

Both sides being anxious to join battle, tariffs moved to center stage. As the GOP's most effective spokesman for industrialization and high wages, McKinley was spotlighted. Not a few party leaders began to rate him a better 1888 presidential prospect than Ohio's favorite son Sherman, whom McKinley was committed to support.

At the 1888 national convention, McKinley once again chaired the resolutions committee, well placed to build enthusiasm. His potential as a dark horse was open conversation. However, on the fourth ballot—after his support on the third had climbed to eight votes—when a Connecticut delegate vote for McKinley suggested unwelcome momentum, the Ohio congressman interrupted the roll call for a personal insistence:

> In the presence of the duty resting on me, I cannot remain silent with honor. I cannot, consistently with the wish of the state whose credentials I bear and which has trusted me; I cannot, consistently with my own views of personal integrity, consent, or seem to consent, to permit my name to be used as a candidate before this convention. . . . I do not request—I demand, that no delegate who would not cast reflection upon me shall cast a ballot for me.[3]

If the 1884 convention had given McKinley stature, the events of 1888 burnished it. Home-state Sherman supporters praised his fidelity, and Mark Hanna, then only a state-level power broker, was impressed enough to switch his factional allegiance and fund-raising ability from Governor Foraker to McKinley. A year later, when

Foraker lost his bid for a third statehouse term, McKinley became Ohio's next-in-line presidential favorite son. In declining to gamble for the nomination in 1888, he may well have perceived that in his mid-forties and able to wait, he could and should reject a late-ballot Hayes- or Garfield-type nomination lacking any grassroots underpinning. Harrison, victor on the eighth ballot, found that out over his four years.

Selfless or Machiavellian, McKinley's new prestige brought numerous benefits. In the House, he was put up for Speaker in 1889 and lost by a single vote to Thomas B. Reed of Maine. His appeal to rank-and-file GOP House members proven, McKinley was named chairman of the Ways and Means Committee and Republican floor leader. And because Harrison's victory over Cleveland meant GOP trade promises to fulfill, McKinley as Ways and Means chairman would lead this effort during the 1889–90 Congress.

Tariff politics reached its greatest crescendo between 1880, when Garfield turned it into a Republican electoral sword, and 1897, when McKinley resolved the basic debate in the GOP's favor. As the United States became the leading world industrial power, interest groups locked horns for unprecedented stakes. Cleveland couldn't get even a Democratic Congress to abandon the principle of protection in 1893, although some rates were selectively reduced. Republican Congresses, for their part, couldn't put through new tariff schedules while Cleveland was in the White House (1885–89, 1893–97). The two major tariff enactments of this period—the McKinley Tariff of 1890 and the Wilson-Gorman Tariff Act of 1894—are both best understood as way stations to the resolution of the tariff question in the 1896 election and its legislative aftermath.

Tariff politics became even more of a minefield in 1889 and 1890 through the admission of six new western states—North Dakota, South Dakota, Wyoming, Montana, Idaho, and Utah. While giving the Republicans more long-term strength in the Senate, in the short run, these admissions created a new bloc of silver-state GOP solons anxious to renegotiate national economic policy. Western support for protectionism now had two conditions: first, a full range of tariff protection for agricultural and livestock products, as well as manufactures; second, enactment of further legislation to increase silver's role in the U.S. money supply.

Such were the complications in 1889 and 1890 when for the first time since 1875, a Republican president also had a Republican Congress.[4] At the same time, the Gilded Age economy, with its money wars and overleveraged stocks, was slipping toward the great depression of the mid-nineties. The first tremors came in the recession of 1890. Autumn saw the U.S. money markets tremble in the wake of British financial jitters, causing dozens of Eastern bank and brokerage firm failures. These, in turn, inhibited the crop-season flow of money from Eastern banks westward, where grain production was already parched by severe drought and nascent Populism was spreading like a prairie fire. The peak of financial skittishness, overlapping the midterm elections, came in October and early November, when the prominent London firm of Barings suspended payments. Still, this slide was short and U.S. economic recovery came by mid-1891.

This is not unnecessary economic embroidery. Part of the institutional weakness of the presidency between 1872 and 1896 reflected the devastation wrought by recessions on the chief executive's party in Congress. The midterm elections of 1874, 1878, and 1882 were painful enough. Those of 1890 and 1894, however, would hand the party in the White House even worse—a blistering 78 House seats lost by the Republicans in 1890, an almost unbelievable 117 torn from the Democrats in 1894.

The newly enacted McKinley Tariff of 1890 was one of the reasons for that year's heavy GOP losses. Even though its rate schedules had taken effect only on October 6, some merchants were quick to prematurely raise prices on items in stock, and clever Democrats took this mercantile proclivity and magnified it. In McKinley's own district, tin peddlers were hired to go into rural districts offering coffeepots and tin cups at ridiculous prices, blaming the McKinley Tariff. Elsewhere, the exaggeration was more routine.

The spending excesses of the "Billion Dollar" Republican Congress—overfattened veterans' pensions, in particular—were another drag. Even so, the GOP's biggest problem was economic and financial—the middling panic in the East and the combination of drought, third-party Populism, and hard times in the Midwest and West. Dry and angry Kansas, which had given the Republicans all seven of its House seats in 1888, dumped five for Populists in 1890. Other large losses came in big states like Massachusetts, New York, Ohio, and Illinois.

In Ohio, though, the Republican ebb was notably intensified by the Democratic legislature's gerrymander. They created a half dozen lopsidedly GOP districts (out of twenty-one) in order to improve another half dozen from marginally Republican to marginally Democratic. As we have seen, most notable artistry was in McKinley's district, redrawn to yield a normal Democratic margin of 3,000 votes, which his popularity and effort kept down to a 302-vote Democratic edge.

Few Ohio observers singled out the tariff. Friendly commentators bemoaned partisan manipulation. The statistically minded weighed McKinley's strength in clearly Democratic territory and named him a probable winner against Democratic Governor James E. Campbell in the next gubernatorial election twelve months away. In Ohio, the Cleveland *Leader* opined that "the result makes Major McKinley the next governor of Ohio," and the *Columbus Dispatch* agreed. Similar points were made by the *New York Tribune*, the *Pittsburgh Gazette*, the *Philadelphia Record*, and the *Chicago Inter-Ocean*.[5]

In the spring of 1891, a delegation of Ohioans sent to Washington succeeded in convincing McKinley, still in town for the lame-duck session of Congress, to make the statehouse run. Because a loss to Campbell could end his career, he had thought about waiting until 1892 and gaining reelection to Congress. However, the economy showed new life and the recession's lifting in midsummer cleared away that voter grudge. An enthusiastic 1891 GOP state convention nominated McKinley by acclamation. Then his gubernatorial margin of 21,000 votes, roughly what experts foresaw from his House showing, was substantial for that era of close division. It was better, for example, than Rutherford Hayes had ever managed in his three Ohio gubernatorial victories.

Returning to the House in the next election might well have narrowed McKinley, trapping him in a legislative mind-set, as it did his once and future rival, Speaker Thomas Reed. Instead, William McKinley, Jr., as he still appeared on Ohio ballots, took up a position that, despite its limited administrative clout, sidestepped

Washington tariff backbiting and promised a Republican, who was already well known nationally, new executive credentials and a further push toward the presidency.

THE GOVERNOR, ANTIMACHINE POLITICS, AND THE 1896 NOMINATION

McKinley's powerful capture of the 1896 Republican presidential nomination followed a relative nonchalance—activity that scarcely rose above intra-GOP image building—with respect to the 1892 nomination. President Harrison sought renomination for a second term. Most party leaders, however, doubted his chances. They also doubted, should Harrison be pushed aside, that any other Republican could win in what looked to be a poor year. By the spring of 1892, with the economy seemingly renewed, large portions of the Eastern financial community were already lining up behind a second term for conservative Democrat Grover Cleveland, whom Harrison had unseated four years earlier. Few expected any Republican nominee to carry Eastern swing states like New York, New Jersey, and Connecticut.

It was not, in short, a nomination worth fighting for. Mark Hanna, free to boost McKinley now that Sherman was out, went to the GOP national convention in Minneapolis. Supposedly, he wanted to block Harrison's renomination on the first ballot so that a divided convention might turn to McKinley. McKinley's arrival added to the boomlet; biographers agree that his mere appearance in many places brought applause.[6]

But the governor was merely showing his flag. Push was not intended to come to shove. In his official role as 1892 convention chairman, McKinley performed impartially and lavishly praised Harrison. When Ohio cast all but one of its delegate votes for favorite son McKinley, the one was McKinley's own proxy, conspicuously cast for Harrison. When the incumbent was renominated on the first ballot, it was McKinley who asked that the choice be made unanimous.

Because dissenters blocked agreement, the first ballot total remained divided: Harrison 535, Blaine 182½, and McKinley 182. This indifference to unity was not the only poor augury. New York boss Thomas Platt joked about his delegates wrapping themselves in furs to ward off the chill of Harrison's renomination and returning home to await defeat (a good forecast, inasmuch as Cleveland's 45,000-vote statewide majority in New York would be the largest to date for a Democratic presidential nominee). The two dissenting blocs left on the tally sheet were the party's fond wave to the past— to its "plumed knight," James G. Blaine—and its nod to better prospects under McKinley.

Watching McKinley's skilled 1884–96 ascent of Mount Nomination is impressive, a bit like seeing a first-rate climber move across a particularly challenging rock face. No other nineteenth-century Republican ever advanced so methodically, but careful preparation was a McKinley talent dating back to his wartime staff work.

Cleveland unseated Harrison in 1892 by enough—carrying Wisconsin and even coming close in New Hampshire—that by his inauguration, some Democrats believed the twenty-year logjam of national politics had broken in their favor. In May and June, however, with the unlucky Cleveland only some ten weeks in office, they were humbled by the decade's main economic earthquake, for which the shudders of 1890 had been only a mild precursor.

The great depression of 1893 to 1897, a political prop first to McKinley's rise to the presidency and then, through its timely finish, to his success in office, was one of the two or three deepest in U.S. history. Overextended railroads, weighed down by watered stocks and bonds, led the crash. Banks and farm prices followed. Farm destitution and general unemployment swelled enough that in 1893, the Populist governor of Kansas, Lorenzo Lewelling, issued his famous Tramp Circular, likening the jobless men on the roads to the social unrest of Tudor England and prerevolutionary France.

McKinley himself was fortunate to be in Ohio. The defeat that had taken him from Washington's economic and tariff cockpit led to a major statehouse platform on which to display his reformist and labor credentials. As one biographer noted, "He permitted the tariff issue to slumber until hard times after 1893 made him the prophet of prosperity."[7] His record, together with the popular economic reaction against Cleveland and the Democrats, reelected him in 1893 with the highest share of the total vote given any Ohio governor since the Unionist coalition of the Civil War.

Ironically, he had to survive his own brief brush with the economic downturn. He had endorsed notes for an old friend and schoolmate, Robert Walker, in the amount—or so McKinley thought—of some $17,000.[8] Already successful, Walker was starting a tin-plate business. When he went bankrupt in 1893, supposedly with a liability of $25,000 or so, McKinley cut short a trip and returned to Ohio. His plan, he told assembled friends like Mark Hanna, William R. Day, Herman Kohlsaat, and banker Myron Herrick (himself later governor), was to resign the governorship and resume the practice of law. Within a day or two, as banks were contacted by his friends, McKinley's obligation turned out to rise to $60,000 and finally $130,000.

Mrs. McKinley's $70,000 estate from her father was in her name and not reachable, but she insisted on pledging it to help. Hanna, making the arrangements, allowed her to deed it to him in escrow "to be used if needed." The governor also insisted on turning over his properties to trustees. Convinced not to resign, for the moment, he rejected the suggestion of raising funds through a public subscription. He accepted the services of his friends as trustees in consolidating the debt, but told them that he expected to pay it himself. Instead, they raised the money from private contributors, mostly in Cleveland, Pittsburgh, and Chicago, and paid off the cosigned notes so that McKinley—by now, the probable next president—did not need to go back to practicing law.

Hanna, Herrick, and the others involved appear to have been careful. McKinley was kept from knowing the names of most of the contributors, aside from the close friends who were trustees. None appear to have sought favors or accepted offices. Few Democratic politicians directly challenged the propriety, usually confining themselves to noting that the governor was not a good businessman or that he couldn't take care of his own affairs.

In 1893, this did not do the damage it might have in another year. The public was sympathetic. Voluntary public offerings received at the governor's office alone exceeded the $130,000 needed, although they were all returned. During that autumn's gubernatorial campaign, the miners McKinley had defended without charge in 1876 came to see him; they wanted to help by paying the money he had earlier refused. Here is biographer Leech's conclusion:

His trouble had awakened strong sympathy, not only for a kindly man whose trust had been betrayed, but for an honest politician who had not used public office for personal gain. The whole circumstance of McKinley's bankruptcy and the liberality of his friends became, as the Democratic *Brooklyn Eagle* later commented, "a matter of hearthstone pleasure around the land."[9]

Despite easy reelection as governor, McKinley still had to leap a few hurdles and reconfirm his popular appeal at key points in the 1896 nominating process. Even so, Mark Hanna seems to have been fundamentally correct in his earlier assessment of the 1892 convention: "The demonstration at Minneapolis convinced me that, although it was an impolitic thing for his interests to nominate him there, in the next national convention the popular demand for his candidacy would override all opposition."[10]

In the economic depths of 1894, McKinley took to the national hustings, flailing Cleveland and the Democrats for unsettling business in 1892 with their free-trade promises. These fears, he said, had been removed only in 1894 when the Democratic Wilson-Gorman Tariff Act kept protective policies in place after all. As an economic explanation of the downturn, the tariff uncertainty was probably peripheral. However, given the Democrats' exaggerations in their own 1890 tariff rhetoric, McKinley's barnstorming was fair retribution. He gave 371 speeches in three hundred cities before some two million people during the 1894 campaign, visiting many of the districts where Republicans gained House seats. The outcome strengthened his hand for the 1896 nomination.

What suspense remained came from uncertainties in the all-important Midwest. Forgoing reelection as governor to be free to politick in 1896, a careless McKinley lost control of the June 1895 Ohio GOP convention to the rival faction headed by ex-governor Foraker. The McKinley and Foraker factions thereupon made a loose compact: McKinley would back the faction's candidate, Asa Bushnell, for governor in 1895 and Foraker for U.S. senator in 1896, and those two, in office, would keep the Ohio party solidly behind McKinley's presidential ambitions.

In consequence, McKinley spent little of 1895 on the national stage and more at home supporting Bushnell and the local GOP contenders whose victories would ensure a pro-Foraker legislature. His broader task, in a nutshell, was to display enough hold on the Ohio electorate to bind Foraker and Bushnell to him during 1896. Huge crowds duly came forth, including miners and factory workers. Bushnell's healthy 51 percent of the gubernatorial vote was not far below McKinley's own 52.6 percent in 1893, and the deal was set. Foraker, elected to the Senate by a solidly Republican legislature in early 1896, would work for McKinley's nomination.

Ohio aside, McKinley and Hanna were able to reject deals. In late 1895, as the party chieftains saw the Ohioan heading toward nomination, the two most important Eastern leaders, Senator Matthew Quay of Pennsylvania and ex-Senator Thomas Platt of New York (soon to be senator again), met with Hanna. Their price for convention support was at least one cabinet seat; Platt was set on becoming secretary of the Treasury and demanded the commitment in writing.

Hearing these terms from Hanna, McKinley is said to have replied: "There are some things in this world that come too high. If I cannot be president without promising to make Tom Platt Secretary of the Treasury, I will never be president."[11] Parenthetically, Hayes, Garfield, and Harrison had all drawn the line at giving the Treasury to an Easterner. McKinley would have looked like a chump to agree.

But no deal was necessary. Quay, Platt, and their allies had no strong rival to field. Their favorite, the preferred nominee of the East, was House Speaker Thomas Reed of Maine, a three-hundred-pound procorporate conservative with little following west of the Appalachians. To brake McKinley's advance, they decided to deploy a group of favorite-son candidates: Reed in New England, Governor Levi P. Morton in New York, Quay himself in Pennsylvania, ex-President Benjamin Harrison (possibly) in Indiana, Senator Shelby Cullom in Illinois, and Senator William B. Allison in Iowa. Together, they might keep a McKinley nomination from jelling.

The first link in this weak chain broke in February when Harrison told Indiana's top McKinley backer, future senator Charles Fairbanks, that he would not be a candidate in 1896. That left Indiana open to Fairbanks and his McKinley activists. March saw the Ohio convention plump for McKinley, with Senator Foraker agreeing to head the delegation. Wisconsin, Minnesota, Nebraska, and South Dakota followed suit. Hanna and McKinley had already lined up most of the Southern delegates, and inroads in Vermont, New Hampshire, and Connecticut broke Reed's hold on New England.

The decisive arena, however, was the Illinois state GOP convention in late April. Its endorsement had to be nailed down for McKinley. Unlike Allison, Quay, and Morton, Cullom's White House potential did not have to be humored. Victory for McKinley in Illinois would comfortably increase his delegate lead, impress the uncommitted, and rebuke the favorite-son plotters. Achieving it fell to a thirty-year-old reformer new to McKinley's campaign staff, Charles G. Dawes. Thirty years later, Dawes would become vice president of the United States, but in late April, his first moment in the national political sun came from beating Shelby Cullom and the Illinois and Chicago machines.

Cullom tried to bargain, but Dawes recalled many years later in his book *A Journal of the McKinley Years* that he heard the soon-to-be president tell Cullom "that he proposed to take the place, if it came to him, unmortgaged."[12] Dawes had his own goal: "to make the machine sick before we get through with them."[13] He succeeded, and the Illinois endorsement of McKinley was widely regarded as sewing up the nomination. The national convention in St. Louis was by then just seven weeks away.

A week before it opened, Joseph Manley, the Maine GOP boss and strategist for Speaker Reed, threw in the towel: McKinley, he acknowledged, would be nominated on the first ballot. The Ohio governor ultimately received 661½ ballots to 84½ for Reed, 61½ for Quay, 58 for Morton, and 35½ for Allison. Not only had the several machines failed to stop McKinley, they had become his foils, his targets of opportunity. Early in 1896, the *New York Herald Tribune* had surmised that should McKinley win, he might "owe his success to the underlying and deep-seated hostility of the mass Republican voters to the dictation and domination of a boss oligarchy."[14]

Senator Francis Warren of Wyoming advised a friend that "McKinley is in it with the masses in nearly every state in the Union . . . The politicians are making a hard fight against him, but if the masses could speak, McKinley is the choice of at least 75% of the entire Republican voters in the Union, and I am not considered much of a McKinley man, either."[15] McKinley, for his part, felt strongly about his popular support, citing it principally as a moral obligation. Mark Hanna, practical and a promoter by nature, turned his friend's discussion of stopping the bosses into a pointed campaign slogan: the campaign of "The People Against the Bosses." Its truth, as we will pursue in chapter 5, picked up further strength from the reform credentials of the state McKinley lieutenants: Dawes and several old Lincolnians in Illinois, Fairbanks (who would be Theodore Roosevelt's vice president) in Indiana, Robert La Follette in Wisconsin, future governor Albert B. Cummins in Iowa, and many others. Kinships like these would bolster McKinley against Bryan's regional appeal to the old Grangers, reformers, and antimachine dissidents.

Before turning to the election and realignment of 1896, it is essential to spell out the relationship between McKinley and Hanna. Its distortion became the principal club with which the pro-Bryan Hearst newspapers, led by the *New York Journal*, sought to bludgeon the Republican ticket. Hearst correspondent Alfred Henry Lewis, seizing on Hanna's role in rescuing McKinley from his 1893 financial problems, used the episode to portray Hanna as the chief of a millionaire syndicate, gambling for the White House, who would "shuffle him [McKinley] and deal him like a pack of cards."[16] More influential still were Homer Davenport's cartoons of Hanna and McKinley, depicting the former as an obese plutocrat, covered with money bags and dollar signs, with McKinley as a smaller puppet, dancing on strings pulled by Hanna. Davenport's caricature, more than Lewis's poison pen, lingered with a vengeance.

Biographers Leech, Morgan, and Gould concur that McKinley, not Hanna, made the important decisions. They employ similar arguments and citations, but Margaret Leech has set out a particularly intriguing psychological explanation:

He [Hanna] had been magnetized by a polar attraction. Cynical in his acceptance of contemporary political practices, Hanna was drawn to McKinley's idealistic standards like a hardened man of the world who becomes infatuated with virgin innocence. That his influence ruled McKinley was the invention of the political opposition, of young Mr. Hearst's newspapers, in particular. Hanna, on the contrary, treated McKinley with conspicuous deference. . . . McKinley gave the orders, Charles G. Dawes noted in his close association with both men, and Hanna obeyed them without question. [Herman] Kohlsaat wrote that Hanna's attitude towards McKinley "was always that of a big, bashful boy toward the girl he loves." Hanna told the story himself. He said that somehow he felt for McKinley an affection that could not be explained, but he explained it very well.[17]

In June 1896, when Hanna followed up the St. Louis convention by visiting McKinley, who had remained in Canton and kept in touch by telephone, both men considered autumn's general election well in hand. True, parts of the Middle West had reacted against the gold plank in the Republican platform. But the Cleveland administration was receiving most of the blame for the economic depression. The Democrats' huge 1894 losses were proof enough. That badly divided party, Republicans assumed, had no strong candidate or issues to rally around. Two weeks later, July's Democratic convention proved them wrong and set the stage for one of America's great electoral battles.

MCKINLEY AND THE REALIGNMENT OF 1896

Historians disagree over how many observers anticipated the 1896 Democratic convention's nomination of thirty-six-year-old William Jennings Bryan, a former congressman from Nebraska. Apparently not many. Missouri Representative Richard "Silver Dick" Bland had been the spring front-runner. The gold forces allied to the unpopular Cleveland administration had no agreed-upon candidate. In the early months of 1896, Bryan, a long shot, had confided his seemingly implausible hopes only to friends. But in May and June, as the expected convention dominance by silver delegates grew, so did the Nebraskan's quiet campaign.

By the time Bryan arrived in Chicago for early July's convention, he was taken seriously, although not expected to win. However, as a member of the resolutions committee, the Nebraskan staged a coup, arranging a convention debate on the currency issue, with himself as the concluding speaker for silver. The rhetoric, including his famous "cross of gold" allegory, had already been well tested on church, farm, and congressional audiences.[18] This would be his great chance.

Charles Dawes, the young McKinley aide, was an old friend of Bryan's from Nebraska, familiar with his oratory and ambition alike. In his journal for July 7, he set down a prediction to Mark Hanna: if Bryan got a chance to make a speech, he would be nominated. Dawes attended the Democratic convention on the ninth to hear his friend's oratory, which he called "magnificent," despite "pitifully weak" logic.[19] To many Democratic attendees, however, Bryan's words were messianic—a call to arms, not just to oppose the gold standard, but to save democracy and stand again, as Andrew Jackson had stood, against the encroachments of organized wealth. Excitement rippled out of the convention hall and across the nation.

Years later, the Kansas journalist William Allen White would recall that "It was the first time in my life and in the life of a generation in which any man large enough to lead a national party had boldly and unashamedly made his cause that of the poor and oppressed."[20] Not only did Bryan's speech secure him the nomination, but its Jacksonian themes also unnerved Midwestern Republicans, mindful of their own distrust of the East, and threw a weighty stone into the quiet pool of June GOP electoral assumptions.

Mark Hanna canceled a planned European vacation. July's wave of popular pro-Bryan reaction moved the perceived electoral combat zone from the Dakotas, Nebraska, and Kansas—parched, Populist, and by GOP political calculations expendable—hundreds of miles east to the pivotal population concentrations of the Great Lakes: Minnesota, Wisconsin, Illinois, Michigan, Indiana, and Ohio. These essential six counted 97 of the 224 electoral votes needed to elect a president.

In July, Bryan also picked up the endorsement of the Populist party, albeit in a relatively complicated set of circumstances unimportant to this book's examination. In short, the fusion was as much minus as plus. The critical nuance was that although the Midwest had been the cockpit of the Grangers and Greenbackers a decade or two earlier, by 1892, the fires had banked enough that five of the six pivots had given only weak support—from 1.8 percent in Ohio to 4.3 percent in Michigan—to the third-party Populist presidential contender. Only in Minnesota had nominee James Weaver gotten 11.3 percent. By and large, Great Lakes area farmers were more sophisticated and diversified in their crops than the Plains wheat growers. This would turn out to be a vital distinction.

Between mid-July and early September, when Republican leaders began to breathe more easily, large sums were raised for education, mailings, and canvasses—a mobilization doubly designed to rebut Democratic free silver arguments and ensure Republican turnout. Late July had seen Democrats optimistic about a regional sweep. August sampling had Bryan still ahead in Iowa. By early September, Hanna, Dawes, and company found Ohio and Michigan looking better, although pro-silver Iowa remained close. The Middle West, still a battleground, now leaned slightly to the Republicans.

Uncertainty about the East ended in September when the early voting states of Vermont and Maine turned in huge Republican margins reminiscent of the party's Civil War heyday. Such evidence of gold Democrats sulking and GOP voters rallying forecast Bryan's solid defeat in the three Northeastern states that had backed Cleveland in 1892—New Jersey, New York, and Connecticut. Pennsylvania and the rest of New England were safely Republican.

Out West, the three Pacific states of California, Washington, and Oregon teetered. However, the silver bloc—Idaho, Utah, Nevada, Montana, Wyoming, and Colorado—was even more solidly for Bryan than was the South. October's duel would be in the Middle West. Both sides knew it and concentrated their efforts.

Of Bryan's 250 last campaign stops, some 160 were in eight Middle Western states. McKinley, politicking from his own Ohio front porch by receiving all kinds of visiting delegations, wound up with the same regional emphasis. In the end, however, the Middle West voted decisively for McKinley—Ohio, Indiana, Michigan, Illinois, Wisconsin, Minnesota, and Iowa all backed him. The electoral college outcome pivoted accordingly.

Which brings us back to this chapter's initial query: Was the

election and realignment of 1896 personal to McKinley or something that another Republican could have managed? The answer lies
in the voting data: personal to McKinley.

The Ohioan beat Democrat Bryan in the popular count by
7,108,480 votes to 6,511,495 and in the electoral college by 271 to
176. Yet his margin of 596,985 covered up what was in some ways
a closer race. Bryan himself calculated that a change of roughly
20,000 votes in California, Oregon, Kentucky, Indiana, North
Dakota, and West Virginia would have given him a total of 224
electoral votes and the election. "This calculation," he added, "is
made to show how narrow was the defeat of bimetallism and what
is possible for the future."[21] Fraud, while it existed in Illinois and
elsewhere, was not decisive.[22]

In all likelihood, no other Republican could have done as well as
McKinley. Certainly not porcine House Speaker Reed, whose Yankee drawl, acerbic wit, and longtime support for gold would have fit
into an Eastern stereotype to voters west of the Appalachians. Simply subtract from McKinley's total the reasonably close states of
California, Oregon, Indiana, Ohio, and North Dakota—all political
cultures where Reed's Eastern orientation would have played into
Bryan's hands—and the House Speaker would have been defeated.
Probably he would not have done that well.

New York Governor Levi Morton, a stiff seventy-two-year-old
banker who had been Benjamin Harrison's little-noticed vice president, would have been even weaker. Among those favored by the
machine chiefs, the most plausible winner was Iowa Senator
William B. Allison. Respected in the Senate, he had coauthored
major silver legislation in 1878 with Missouri Democratic Congressman "Silver Dick" Bland. Despite his age (sixty-seven) and lackluster
public persona, he might have been able to hold most of the Midwest. If so, Quay, Platt, and the other Eastern leaders presumably
could have carried their own bailiwicks for Allison against a Bryan
caricatured as a lineal descendant of Marat and Robespierre.

Probing within the Middle West, however, identifies a whole range
of McKinley singularities and personal credentials that buoyed him
with urban voters, labor, Catholics, Germans, Union veterans, and his
native region's currency bimetallists. If Bryan sought to reclaim an
agricultural, rural America—his revivalist speech to the Democratic

convention contended that "the great cities rest on our broad and fertile prairies. Burn down your cities and leave our farms, and your cities will spring up again as if by magic; but destroy our farms and the grass will grow in the streets of every city in the country"—McKinley appealed to a very different industrialized, urbanized America.

His vista of prosperity conjoined protective tariffs, sound money, and skilled immigrants from Europe flocking to factory jobs that paid wages twice those of Düsseldorf, Bradford, or Milan. He could discuss those wage relationships like no other leading political figure, and in the last weeks of the campaign, he increasingly focused on job and tariff issues and public praise for labor.

From Boston to San Francisco, virtually every major Northern city backed McKinley, often reversing normal Democratic majorities. In states like Maryland, Illinois, and California, his statewide victory margins came on tidal waves from Baltimore, Chicago, and San Francisco. In his own Ohio, the six largest counties, including Cuyahoga (Cleveland) and Hamilton (Cincinnati), carried for Democrat Grover Cleveland by a slim margin of 1,800 votes in 1892, produced a 31,000-vote margin for McKinley. This was almost half of his statewide lead. In New York, unprecedented Republican vote totals were paced by huge urban gains, including a GOP sweep of New York City's crowded ethnic sidewalks—a telling tabulation of what drove the *New York Journal* to its character distortions.

Not since Lincoln, who publicly upheld unions and the right to strike during the Civil War, had a Republican nominee so embraced labor. As chapter 2 has profiled, McKinley's career commitment ranged from his early unpaid legal help for arrested miners and his mid-1880s advocacy in Congress of a national system of labor arbitration to later success as governor in enacting Ohio legislation to impose fines and jail sentences on employers who refused to permit employees to join unions.

Jobs were the commitment to which McKinley could always rise. In pledging "the full dinner pail," he could add detailed information about how the tariffs on tinplate or steel rails had moved thousands of jobs from Britain to America and make the data come alive to his audience. During the 1891 gubernatorial race, when incumbent Democrat James Campbell, unschooled on trade issues, charged that a Findlay, Ohio, glassworks benefiting from tariff protection hired mostly Belgians, who were unnaturalized aliens, McKinley was in Findlay the next day to refute the charges. Wages in Ohio, he demonstrated, were three to six times higher than Belgian pay for the same skills, and of the 10 percent of the local glassworkers who were Belgians, nearly all had become citizens.[23]

Religious and cultural ecumenicalism added to his urban, labor, and immigrant appeal. In Ohio, he had aligned with the Hayes, Garfield, and Sherman wing of the party, which usually sidestepped controversial religious, moral, and social issues to emphasize tariffs, jobs, wages, and economic development. In McKinley's case, it helped that Stark County was a Democratic-leaning urban center heterogeneous in religion and home to large Irish and German populations. Tolerance was necessary politics when your home district included sizable blocs of Catholics, Methodists, Lutherans, Quakers, and Mennonites.

Bryan, by contrast, had a rural Protestant evangelical mind-set. This led him to insist that "a very great economic question is in reality a great moral question," as well as to liken himself to Old and New Testament figures like David and Saul of Tarsus, while calling for America's spiritual and financial redemption through free coinage of silver. Hoarse at the end of a day's campaigning, Bryan would apologize that "a large portion of my voice has been left along the line of travel, where it is still calling sinners to repentance."[24] To late-nineteenth-century Catholics and immigrants, such language evoked the pietist, moralizing, sometimes bluenosed Protestantism many had come to distrust.

Since the 1850s, the preachy Republican voice in which such morality expressed its usual politics had made Democrats out of the great bulk of Catholics and Lutherans. Their religions, by contrast, were liturgical and ritualistic, and most communicants were uncomfortable with utopias, revivals, redemption, and evangelism. From 1884 to 1892, a wave of Middle West GOP positions against religious schools and for Sunday closings and strict liquor laws had significantly undercut Lutheran and Catholic support for the party, especially among Germans. Thus it was of great importance, in the McKinley versus Bryan race of 1896, that the two parties and presidential nominees had partially reversed their stereotyped roles.

As an Ohio congressman and governor, McKinley had been at odds with the socially combative and somewhat nativist wing of the GOP led by Joseph Foraker. Indeed, the American Protective Association (APA), anti-immigrant and anti Catholic in tenor, worked against McKinley in 1896 for having appointed too many Catholics to office in Ohio. One social historian summarized as follows:

> Numerous local councils of the order in Ohio enacted resolutions declaring their opposition to him. In April, the National Advisory Board announced that it had investigated the charges brought against McKinley by APA leaders, viz., that he had discriminated in his appointments in favor of Romanists and against American Protestants and found them to be accurate. The Board also drew attention to the number of prominent Catholics who had announced their support for McKinley. In early May, both the Executive Committee and the Campaign Committee of the order issued public statements opposing McKinley, and announced their willingness to accept any other potential Republican candidate.[25]

Meanwhile, the GOP presidential nominee enjoyed the open support of Archbishop John Ireland of St. Paul (Minnesota), a blunt critic of Bryan and Populism and arguably the most influential Catholic prelate in the Midwest. After Ireland and McKinley collaborated in the 1896 campaign, including tactics for dealing with the APA, the archbishop subsequently served in an informal diplomatic role for the Vatican, trying to prevent Spain and the United States from going to war in 1898. A leader in the Jansenist or mildly puritan (and prohibitionist) wing of Irish-American Catholicism, he helped candidate McKinley with the St. Paul Irish. He had much less effect with the beer-garden German Catholics in small-town Minnesota whose trends merely matched the Great Lakes norm.

On Election Day, Catholics in the United States, no more than 25–30 percent Republican in the 1892 presidential election, probably cast some 40–45 percent of their vote for McKinley. This is the surmise of scholars like Richard Jensen, Paul Kleppner, and others, although precise data do not exist. Besides swelling the huge Northern urban tides, the GOP Catholic gains also spilled over into

rural sections, into upper Midwest locales that were almost European in how their transplanted German, Belgian, Dutch, Bohemian,
and Slavic towns clumped around towering church spires visible
for miles. Townships like these generally gave McKinley 10–20 percent more of their vote than Harrison had won. Whereas in the
East, the broader anti-Bryan shift was so large that New York, New
Jersey, and Connecticut would have gone Republican easily even
with no change in Catholic loyalties, that was not true in the hard-
fought Middle West. There, the 1892–96 Catholic swing, interwoven with a hard-to-separate urban shift, was decisive.

Across the Middle West, Lutherans—German Lutherans, in particular—were scarcely less important. Between 1870 and 1890, the
Yankee Protestant share of the region's vote had declined as immigration increased the Catholic and Lutheran electorates. Wisconsin
in 1890 was 35 percent Catholic and 30 percent Lutheran, Ohio 25
percent Catholic and 25 percent Lutheran, and Michigan 20 percent Catholic and 15 percent Lutheran.[26] Ignoring these demo-
graphic tides in the 1880s had undercut the GOP; in 1896, the
miscalculation would be Bryan's. McKinley had learned from Ohio
how important the German vote was, and in 1896, his national
campaign had a German division, which wooed both Catholics and
Lutherans.

In one tabulation, the fifteen most populous counties in the Midwest, 40 percent of their voters liturgical Germans, gave McKinley
56.6 percent of their vote while the rest of the region gave him only
53 percent. His share of the German vote, Catholic and Lutheran,
might have been 50–55 percent, up from Harrison's 30–40 percent
in 1892. The *Illinois Staats-Zeitung* made this assessment:

> The German voters decided the [1896] election in Ohio, Indi-
> ana, Michigan, Illinois, Wisconsin, Iowa, Nebraska and Min-
> nesota. . . . They have many complaints against the Republican
> party, which . . . sought to combat the influence of Germans in
> every way, and annoyed them continually with Prohibition
> laws, Sunday closing laws and school laws. The Germans conse-
> quently turned their backs on the Republicans, with the result
> that Cleveland was twice elected, and if the Democrats had not
> inscribed repudiation, bankruptcy and dishonor on their colors

as a result of the union with the Populists, the Germans would have supported them this time also. . . .[27]

By 1896, the Hayes-Garfield-Sherman-McKinley wing of the Ohio GOP had learned from experience about balancing German *biergartens* and parochial schools against Protestant moral crusades. Garfield, a former college professor who spoke German, had held open house, greeting arrivals with "Alles wilkommen." Sherman reminisced in his memoirs about liking to make a Sunday stop at a German beer garden in Cincinnati "to see the people enjoy themselves, to drink a glass of that good old German beverage, beer, and to listen to the music."[28] No possible Eastern party nominee had a comparable regional feel.

McKinley, too, had eased away from his earlier prohibitionist inclinations, by the 1890s taking the occasional glass of wine (and even the occasional Scotch whisky). However, although he didn't visit beer gardens, he was well acquainted with other Teutonic traits: how Germans from Minnesota to Ohio had generally stayed aloof from morally fervent Great Plains Populism and equally distrusted the inflationary panaceas of silver. The German government, as many of the immigrants from Prussia or Westphalia well knew, had abandoned silver in the early 1870s.

Within the Democratic party, German-Americans helped keep the 1896 Minnesota, Wisconsin, and Michigan Democratic conventions behind gold, a prelude to Election Day's shift to McKinley. In heavily German Milwaukee, when a Populist congressional candidate argued that it did not matter whether money was made of "gold, silver, paper, sauerkraut or sausage," he was laughed off the stage. Several Democratic newspapers, anguished by Bryan's weakness, fell back on warning that Republicans wanted to outlaw beer. The city's top German wards gave McKinley 59 percent of their vote.[29] The small but significant National (Gold) Democratic third-party presidential ticket got only 133,000 votes across the country, but helped McKinley win not just in the Middle West, but in Kentucky and less directly in West Virginia and Maryland.

In specifically endorsing gold in the Republican platform only at the last minute, even McKinley's timing was skillful. His career bimetallism had already enabled him to attract the convention delegates from a number of silver-minded Western states, helping to ensure his first-ballot nomination. Acquiescence to the word *gold* in April or May would have made those inroads impossible. Worse, preconvention gold-silver tensions would have had dangerous weeks to fester among bimetallism-attuned voters in Iowa, Illinois, Indiana, and even Ohio. But when gold language was accepted under pressure in the final days, only the core silver state delegations were angry enough to walk out, and their departure had been inevitable. The nominee's record of bimetallism, plus his repeated commitment to an international conference to remonetize silver, kept pragmatic Republican silverites in line. So did Western GOP support for regionally important tariffs on wool, copper, lumber, and other commodities.

On the Democratic side of the ledger, the GOP platform's commitment to gold came in time to be a summer and autumn beacon to German and other sound-money Democrats repelled by Bryan and free silver coinage at sixteen to one. In the three Midwestern states where local Democratic conventions stuck by gold, German and Catholic Democrats swung to the GOP in much greater numbers than Protestant Republican pietists and evangelicals moved the other way.

If Bryan was strong in the sections of Ohio, Indiana, Illinois, and Iowa disproportionately populated by Southern Baptists, Disciples of Christ, and Cumberland Presbyterians (Bryan's denomination), most of these counties were normally Democratic. However, he also made inroads in some Republican sections of the Middle West populated by the sort of evangelical Protestants who had flocked to earlier-nineteenth-century enthusiasms ranging from abolition and prohibition to perfectionism and millenarianism.

Insistent moralizers were a problem McKinley had earlier faced in Ohio. His ethnic and religious ecumenicalism, his wine, tobacco, and card playing, the relaxation of his staunch Methodism, and his moderate faction's control of the Ohio GOP all provoked dissatisfaction. Besides American Protective Association activists, it came from peripheral elements of the rival Foraker faction and antiliquor stalwarts, some of whom moved into the ranks of Ohio's small but pesky Prohibition party. In 1896, McKinley lost ground in towns and counties where the dissidents collaborated with pro-Bryan groups like the Populists and Farmers Alliance. In the eight Ohio counties where Methodists predominated, McKinley dropped almost a point below Harrison's support in 1888, whereas in the state as a whole he climbed by 2.3 percent, thanks to urban voters.[30] McKinley also slipped in the counties that were the most rural and held the fewest immigrants.

In Ohio and Indiana, the two closest Middle Western states in 1896, the areas where Bryan gained over Cleveland's 1892 showings tended to be units where 1) third-party Populist support had been greatest in 1892 (it now moved largely to Bryan) or 2) concentrations of evangelical or pietist Republicans embraced another crusade for redemption and morality, this time to be held in a prairie Democratic tent. Even with McKinley's net increases in both states, 10,000 votes would have changed the outcome in Indiana and 25,000 in Ohio.

The biggest surprise came in Michigan, a more volatile state with a two-decade history of giving 8–15 percent of its vote to Greenback, Populist, and Prohibition splinter parties. Bryan's redemptionist rhetoric drove large numbers of Catholics and Lutherans toward McKinley. However, it also encouraged the old Yankee core of southern Michigan—abolitionist, food faddist, Seventh Day Adventist, and so on, including the city of Jackson, the GOP's 1854 birthplace—to chalk up Bryan's banner Midwest gains. In contrast to Yankee-settled regions farther east, Michigan Yankee counties had been friendly to Greenbackers and Populists and showed the biggest Bryan trends.

Southern Michigan aside, however, McKinley's Middle West losses of this sort were not large. Despite his softer Methodism, by all but zealots' standards, he remained a born-again true believer. Sydney Ahlstrom, in his magisterial *Religious History of the United States*, called the election of 1896 "one of the great revelatory events in American religious history. As in no other election, both candidates virtually personified American Protestantism. Both William Jennings Bryan and William McKinley were reared in pious homes, educated in denominational colleges and guided throughout their lives by the traditions and practices of evangelism."[31] Among plausible Republican nominees, McKinley had the greatest capacity to limit Bryan's Midwest evangelical inroads.

The Ohioan also had another unique credential. The men who had worn Union blue were beginning to die off in the 1890s, but they remained a large group—usually at least two-to-one Republican—and William McKinley had a rare claim on their affections. While he would be the last American president to have served in the Civil War, he would be the first to have fought part of that war as a private soldier. The election turnout in the Middle West was huge in 1896, and Republicans called upon the Grand Army of the Republic to show that veterans' patriotism demanded the rejection of Bryan. October 31 was declared "Flag Day," with marches in every Northern city.[32] On November 3, the onetime private of the Twenty-third Ohio Volunteer Infantry was chosen as commander in chief.

Despite what became a twentieth-century stereotype of Bryan's cranky economics and rustic evangelism, he was not that easily beaten. In the critical Middle West, McKinley's victory depended enough on his local background, ecumenicalism, and connections that any Eastern nominee would have been weaker. Ironically, the twin dismissals of Bryan and McKinley—the hick and the hack—that became fashionable in the twentieth century may have depended on each other. If Bryan was basically just an agrarian Bible thumper with quack economics, then of course he could have been beaten by a small-town mediocrity who took his marching orders from the Wall Street puppet masters.

The reality is otherwise. In an America where religion was still at the core of national culture, McKinley and Bryan were both in their ways remarkable men—tribunes of the people, not the interests—and their clash shook their home region, in particular. When the dust settled, America's urban and industrial future was narrowly victorious, but many of the reforms Bryan had held out eventually became law under more sedate auspices, a worthy tribute. American electoral politics, in turn, realigned for a generation around the broad outlines (if not the precise patterns) put down in 1896 and 1900 by William McKinley. In the heartland from which both men hailed—in counties named Miami, Wabash, Sangamon, Muscatine, Blue Earth, Fond du Lac, and Traverse—nobody else on the Republican side could have countered enough of Bryan's own moral commitment, proud regionalism, and appeal to the ordinary citizen.

However, before we turn from electoral politics to a larger view of McKinley's success in domestic and economic policy and his place in the annals of both progressivism and the presidency, foreign policy requires attention. It is in this arena that many historians concede that the twenty-fifth president worked a *second* realignment: the expansion of the U.S. role in international affairs and America's transition into the twentieth century as a world power with powerful alliances and rivalries.

4

McKinley and America's Emergence as a World Power

The [Spanish-American] War itself was small, glamorous, a thing of charging rough riders and flashing sabers to many. It was relatively cheap to all save those who suffered and died. But its consequences were far-reaching. Placid, insular America was gone. "No war in history has accomplished so much in so short a time with so little loss," wrote Ambassador Horace Porter from Paris. "The nation has at a bound gone forward in the estimation of the world more than we would have done in fifty years of peace," said Senator [Redfield] Proctor. 　　　　　H. Wayne Morgan, *America's Road to Empire*

For all that he had never been abroad, William McKinley did not enter the White House as a novice in global relations. His years in Congress had produced a wide acquaintance with foreign tariffs, trade, industry, and wage scales. The politics of credibly pursuing an international agreement on currency bimetallism kept him conversant with British, French, German, and other national positions respecting gold and silver. As governor of Ohio and a potential presidential candidate, he followed foreign policy issues through a daily set of clippings from major newspapers, widely recognized as among the era's best sources of information on international developments. Visitors to his office in Columbus sometimes caught him reading books on tariffs.

International references were common in his speeches, and politicians were often surprised at how much he knew. Massachusetts Senator Henry Cabot Lodge, visiting in December 1896, afterward told a friend that "his whole attitude of mind struck me as serious, broad in view, and just what we ought to desire."[1] According to one biographer, "[T]hroughout his presidency, men seemed to be surprised when McKinley showed himself to be well-informed on international bimetallism, the annexation of Hawaii, the tariff laws of the nation's trading partners, or the currents of world politics generally."[2]

Somewhat ironically, historians have been more willing to credit McKinley with foreign rather than domestic policy achievement. They usually cite his prominence as a hinge president—the prime decision maker during America's rise to world power. From 1897 to 1901, he presided over the fruition of the Northern or Yankee version of U.S. expansionism, a commercial manifest destiny tied to increasing American exports. The surge in those exports was little short of stunning—a near doubling from $833 million in 1896 to $1.488 billion in 1901. The successful conduct of the war with Spain, itself a milestone of U.S. alliance building, foreign policy transformation, and new popular global interest, owed much to the skill for staff work and military planning that had made young Major McKinley a divisional chief of staff at twenty-two.

In the White House, he helped to shape and preview America's early-twentieth-century alliances and hostilities: on one hand, entente with Britain and an off-and-on commitment to the territorial integrity of China, and on the other, mounting Caribbean and Pacific tensions with Germany and Japan. Often, as one century ends, some contours of the next appear. So it was in 1898 and 1899. McKinley's further ability to implement military reforms, establish executive office telephone and telegraph communications, display the utility of presidential commissions in international affairs, and enlarge the White House staff helped create an institutional capacity frequently described as the first "modern presidency."

WESTWARD, HO: THE ORIGINS OF YANKEE EXPANSIONISM

Far from emerging in the 1898 seizure of Puerto Rico, Guam, and the Philippines from a defeated Spain, American territorialism was as old as the rapacity of its seventeenth-century colonial settlements. Just as the English revolutionary government of Oliver Cromwell had goals in the Caribbean to match any king's, Cromwell's Puritan cousins in Massachusetts Bay pushed their political ambitions and territory north into what is now Maine and New Hampshire, while angling for much of current-day Rhode Island. Mid-eighteenth-century invasions sailed from Boston to eject the French from what soon became Nova Scotia, and expansionist Massachusetts planted settlements there, too. By the time of the American Revolution, immigrants from Yankee Massachusetts and Connecticut had settled portions of New York, New Jersey, and Pennsylvania and cast their eyes on what would soon be Ohio. By the Civil War, Yankee New England had settled a broad region from the Great Lakes west across the prairie to Washington and Oregon.

Southerners were no less territorially minded. As colonials, they struck at Spanish Florida and in the nineteenth century pushed west across the cotton belt to Texas and the southwest, simultaneously coveting Cuba and a half dozen Mexican states from Sonora to Yucatán. Yankee rivals in Congress blocked Southern hopes of admitting pieces of Mexico and the Caribbean to the Union as slave states, but Dixie's thwarted ambitions had been fierce. For twenty-five years after Lee's surrender at Appomattox, Southerners and Northerners alike were busy filling in the continent until the Western frontier superficially closed in the 1890s. Northern eyes then refocused on a new Pacific frontier that stretched from Alaska, with its beckoning goldfields, to Hawaii, with its New England settlements, and south to Samoa, a favorite stopping place for Yankee sailors even before Herman Melville's Polynesian portraits.

Southerners were less drawn to that frontier, given the Pacific Basin's potential to compete with Dixie in existing crops like cotton, sugar, citrus, hemp, and tobacco. Besides, the push was led by New Englanders who for a century had traded by sailing around Cape Horn and now sought a commercial shortcut across the isthmus of Panama. As the 1890s lengthened, so did the catalogue of Republican-sponsored Pacific expansion: the annexation of Hawaii, stepped-up battleship construction, an Isthmian canal, and, after 1898, control of the Philippines. All won their greatest support in Congress from the Yankee Northeast, Upper Midwest, and Pacific. McKinley pushed all four. The Spanish-American War was only a catalyst. Expansionism was ingrained in the American psyche.

The first independent American voyage to the Orient came in 1784, when the Massachusetts brig *Empress of China* sailed to Canton. This began a commerce that would flower through the 1840s and leave a dozen U.S. cities, including McKinley's in Ohio, named for the great Chinese entry port. By McKinley's inauguration, the American push westward into the Pacific had a long naval and mercantile chronology.

So strategic were the Hawaiian islands by the 1840s that President John Tyler extended the hemispheric shield of the Monroe Doctrine to include them. In 1854, Commodore Matthew Perry visited Japan and negotiated a treaty that opened up the ports of Shimoda, Hakodate, and later Nagasaki to U.S. trade. Perry even urged that the United States take control of Formosa. By that same year, resolutions in Congress to annex Hawaii to the United States began to get serious attention.

The Civil War briefly eclipsed the Orient, but in 1867, U.S. naval expeditions visited Wake Island and occupied Midway—its position was halfway between California and Japan—to establish a coaling station and cable relay. The purchase from Russia in 1867 of Alaska, with its Aleutian island chain pointing toward Asia, pushed American territory even closer to Japan.

In 1871, the U.S. Navy leased facilities in Samoa, and in 1875, the Republican administration of U. S. Grant established trade reciprocity with Hawaii, still at least nominally an independent kingdom. Pago Pago became a naval coaling station in 1879.

Imitating Perry in Japan, U.S. Navy Commodore Robert Shufeldt, under presidential instructions, in 1882 forced Korea to sign a treaty opening itself to American commerce. In 1885, when Hawaii gave the United States exclusive rights to Pearl Harbor as a coaling and naval repair station, President Cleveland called the islands "the stepping-stone to the growing trade of the Pacific." Shufeldt evoked a commercial boudoir: "The Pacific is the ocean bride of America. . . . China and Japan and Korea are the bridesmaids, California is the nuptial couch, the bridal chamber, where all the wealth in the Orient will be brought to celebrate the wedding."[3]

The year 1889 brought a tripartite British, American, and German division of Samoa. January 1893 saw a revolution in Hawaii led by Americans, many of them New Englanders, out to force annexation by the United States. The naval presence of the Germans and Japanese was starting to be a concern.

Expansion in the Pacific was becoming a bone of party contention. In February 1893, Republican President Harrison could not get a treaty annexing Hawaii ratified by the Senate before Democrat Cleveland, inaugurated that March, moved to withdraw it. Cleveland's refusal to take Hawaii, as well as his proposal to abandon Samoa to the British and Germans, became minor 1896 campaign issues. McKinley, after taking office in 1897, resumed the fight to annex Hawaii.

By this point, it is fair to talk of a larger Republican policy loosely including a powerful battleship-led navy, construction of the canal across Nicaragua or Panama, and further stimulus of already burgeoning U.S. exports through trade reciprocity—the so-called bargaining tariff. Foreign access to the U.S. market would be used to persuade the governments of commodity producers, principally in South America, to accept more U.S. manufactured exports in return for selling their commodities. This was a latter-day Hamiltonian vision for the next stage of American industrial development, and its several components became Republican priorities.

Old empires, meanwhile, were tottering. One of Europe's dynastic sick men, the Ottoman Empire, was destabilizing the Balkans as it declined; the senility of a second, imperial Spain hinted at power realignments in the Caribbean and Pacific. The death of Spain's empire could be the birth of an American one, creating a naval and world power better positioned to hold international markets. A band of mostly Republican war hawks including Assistant Secretary of the Navy Theodore Roosevelt, Senator Henry Cabot Lodge, Colonel Leonard Wood, and Navy Captain A. T. Mahan hoped for exactly that.

MCKINLEY AND THE WAR WITH SPAIN

Heeding an 1896 Republican platform that called for Cuban independence, McKinley's firm attitude during 1897 toward Spain's behavior in its Caribbean colony had produced several concessions: the recall to Madrid of the brutal Spanish commander in Cuba,

General Valeriano Weyler, an end to the practice of reconcentration (de facto detention camps), amnesty for political prisoners, and the release of all Americans held in Cuban jails.

But the president, unlike many other Americans, did not leap at war with Spain in order to free Cuba, even after the U.S. battleship *Maine* blew up in Havana harbor one night in February 1898. Not a few in Congress criticized this reluctance. In fact, politics and economics, to say nothing of the usual casualty lists of war in the tropics, made McKinley's reluctance understandable. Incremental pressures on Spain were having measurable results; war had uncertain perils.

Back in 1861, portions of the nation's business and financial community, especially in Boston, New York, and Philadelphia, had considered Lincoln's policies too provocative, worrying that a civil war would disrupt business and cause losses for Northern holders of Southern commercial paper and state bonds. Wartime closure of the Mississippi to North-South commerce did indeed produce enough economic dislocation to hurt Lincoln and the GOP in the Midwest in the 1862 midterm elections. Thirty-six years later, in early 1898, mercantile interests were apprehensive over the potential consequences of the first U.S. war with a European nation since 1812.

Hawkish sentiment in the nation and in Congress, though, was being whipped up by a newer form of enterprise: the major metropolitan newspapers now mushrooming in circulation and anxious to parade their new power. Nevertheless, the reluctance of the broader business and financial communities to fight Spain over Cuba was shared, at least through March 1898, by many House and Senate GOP leaders. Speaker Thomas Reed, Appropriations Committee Chairman Joseph Cannon, and Senators Nelson Aldrich, Oliver Platt, William Allison, and Mark Hanna generally agreed that U.S. pressure eventually would make Spain end its suppression. War was unnecessary.

They also had a practical reservation: that national recovery from the deep 1893 depression could be snuffed out by a war. Despite signs of recovery since summer, the autumn 1897 gubernatorial elections had gone against the GOP. Party candidates lost in Nebraska, New Jersey, New York, and Kansas, and party margins were narrowed in Ohio and Pennsylvania. As we have seen, each Republican administration since Grant's had suffered major midterm losses tied to recessions—in 1874, 1878, 1882, and 1890. Another in 1898, should war prove economically disruptive, could bring in a Democratic Congress and wipe out the programmatic promise of McKinley's solid victory in 1896.

In retrospect, it is easy to say that Spain had to be a pushover. Yet the uncertainties of spring 1898 mixed fear of Spanish attacks on the U.S. East Coast with speculation that other European nations might be drawn to support Spain.[4] At the Navy Department, Theodore Roosevelt had theorized about a U.S. naval attack on Cádiz, even about the fleet entering the Mediterranean to swoop down on Barcelona. Along the East Coast, Americans in the first days of war recalled that as late as the eighteenth century, Spanish warships had threatened Nantucket and Delaware Bay. As war became reality, Portland, Maine, howled for naval protection and Boston bankers toyed with moving their securities to inland Worcester. In Europe, only Britain favored the United States, while Spanish sympathizers in France, Germany, Russia, and Austria-Hungary hinted that if early fighting showed U.S. weakness, demands for a cease-fire and arbitration could be expected. Complications were possible.

In short, caution made sense. However, McKinley was also influenced by a personal distaste. To his White House physician, Leonard Wood, the president remarked, "I shall never get into a war until I am sure God and Man approve. I have been through one war; I have seen the dead piled up; and I do not want to see another." He had said in his inaugural address a year earlier, "We want no wars of conquest; we must avoid the temptation of territorial aggression. War should never be entered upon until every agency of peace has failed; peace is preferable to war in almost every contingency."[5]

His reluctance had an important corollary of emphasis on humanitarian assistance. One example, as we have seen, was the winter help he obtained for the Hocking Valley miners in 1895—partly with his own private funds—after their 1894 strike when troops had been sent in. The needs in Cuba were much greater. Between 1894 and 1896, sugar exports to the United States plummeted, partly because of the sugar tariffs restored in 1894, but also because of the Spanish policy of reconcentrating rebels in cities and camps, leaving the countryside derelict.

In 1897, McKinley sent William Calhoun, one of his political operatives, to Cuba on an inspection tour. He reported back, "I traveled by rail from Havana to Matanzas. The country outside of the military posts was practically depopulated. Every house had been burned, banana trees cut down, canefields swept with fire, and everything in the shape of food destroyed."[6] To Spain, the president protested that fire and famine violated the rules of war. But if the Spanish torched the canefields, so did the rebels. According to one account, Cuban patriot leader Maximo Gomez "destroyed property to keep the issue alive in the United States and to provoke American intervention."[7]

McKinley asked for humanitarian assistance, and in May 1897, Congress responded by appropriating money to assist suffering American citizens in Cuba. Then, in December, McKinley obtained permission from Spain to send food and medicines, and on the day before Christmas, the State Department put out a circular asking for public contributions to a fund for relief to be provided through the American consul in Havana. The president himself anonymously donated five thousand dollars.[8]

His psychologies, meanwhile, were pulled from two sides. What was happening in Cuba was awful. But U.S. war involvement would also have a human cost. Of the troops Spain sent to Cuba in the 1890s, by 1898, some fifty thousand were dead and another fifty thousand disabled by disease and wounds. In 1762, when a British military expedition with a large contingent of American colonial soldiers captured Havana from Spain, the huge casualties had come from disease and debilitation, not the actual fighting.

In mid-March of 1898, business and Wall Street opposition to U.S. military involvement notably softened following a very influential Senate speech by Republican Senator Redfield Proctor, Vermont marble multimillionaire and former secretary of war, following his recent visit to Cuba. Among other things, Proctor noted that of the four hundred thousand Cubans driven into concentration camps, "one half have died and one quarter of the living are so diseased that they cannot be saved."[9] Humanitarian considerations were beginning to gain the upper hand.

As important financiers shifted toward war and the drumbeat from religious publications began to match that of the Yellow Press, Republican politicians sensed a tidal wave. Senator Thomas Platt warned that a Bryan campaign on the issues of "Free Silver and Free Cuba" might carry the 1898 and 1900 elections.[10] Vice President Garret Hobart, whose views McKinley credited, advised, "I can no longer hold back action by the Senate; they will act without you if you do not act at once."[11] When asked if he couldn't stem the bellicosity of the House, Speaker Reed said he might as well "stand out in the middle of a Kansas waste and dissuade a cyclone."[12]

McKinley was losing his options. Biographers agree that the period from February 15, 1898, when the *Maine* exploded, to April 24, when war finally began, was a difficult one for him. Dark circles deepened around his eyes; he needed drugs for sleeplessness. He had hoped, through moderation and diplomatic attention to Spanish *punctilio*, or pride, to convince the government in Madrid that aroused U.S. public and government opinion left Spain no alternative but to withdraw from Cuba.

Foes charged him with vacillation and indecision, of which there was some. But most of his postponements, ambiguities, and hesitations were legitimate. Capital war hawks were infuriated with McKinley's delay and his equivocal language in a March 28 letter sending Congress a naval inquiry board report that the explosion fatal to the battleship *Maine* was external and thus no accident. However, not only Spanish investigators in Cuba but many Americans believed an internal explosion was responsible, among them Fitzhugh Lee, the U.S. consul general in Havana, Captain Sigsbee, the *Maine*'s commanding officer, and most Washington-based U.S. naval officers surveyed by the Washington *Star*.[13]

Ultimately, the skeptics turned out to be correct: the explosion was indeed internal and accidental, caused by a combustion of coal gases, not Spanish wickedness. McKinley must have believed as much, but lacked proof. Open disagreement with the official navy findings would have been impolitic with war fast approaching, not least because of the certain vituperation of the new mass-circulation newspapers. The presumption of the press lords—openly proclaimed by the Hearst press, for example—was that they, not the government, spoke for the American people.

Diplomatic reasons also justified some temporization and delay. The haste by some in Congress to specifically embrace the Cuban revolutionaries, in addition to Cuban independence, was a mistake, and cooler heads on Capitol Hill eventually sided with McKinley's refusal. In April, the president properly delayed hostilities so that Americans had time to leave Cuba. Still another purpose for delay was to give the pro-American British government time to emphasize McKinley's moderation and to smooth the feathers of other European nations inclined to take Spain's side. However, there is a fanciful aspect to the president's later contentions that with a little more time, if Congress had kept quiet, he could have negotiated a satisfactory Spanish exit from Cuba.

No evidence exists that Spanish pride was amenable to that degree of concession; late-twentieth-century historians, including biographers Morgan and Gould, generally agree that the terms communicated to Washington on April 10 spurned U.S. mediation and said nothing of ultimate Cuban independence.[14] This did not constitute acceptance of current McKinley demands. Other scholars have argued that Spanish honor made it necessary for the government in Madrid to fight rather than submit, because "it was an enduring part of Spanish mythology that the empire had been bestowed by God as a reward for the *reconquista*, the liberation of the Iberian Peninsula in 1492 from Islam."[15] On April 11, the president sent Congress a message that put the United States on a two-week pathway to a declaration of war.

Its reception on Capitol Hill was lukewarm, being without trumpets and drum rolls. Of the four reasons listed for intervention, his first was for humanity's sake and to end the devastation of Cuba.[16] Senator Charles Fairbanks later recalled that just prior to the war, McKinley remarked, "I do not care for the property that will be destroyed nor the money that will be expended . . . but the thought of the human suffering that must enter many households almost overwhelms me."[17] William Day, acting secretary of state during the war, told Professor John Bassett Moore of Columbia that for any diplomatic history of the war to be really intelligible, it should discuss the conditions in Cuba and the failure of Spain to better them.[18] These causes were also asserted by senators ranging from Proctor to the leading Southern war backer, Senator John

Morgan of Alabama, and George Hoar of Massachusetts, among the most reluctant Republicans. Biographer Morgan argues that humanitarian considerations were among the scales McKinley most relied upon in coming down on the side of war. If so, this was another unusual facet of an unusual politician.

Militarily, one could argue that the six weeks gained by delays in March and April were vital to increased U.S. naval preparedness. Of the $50 million additional spending for defense voted by Congress in March at the president's request, some $37 million went to the navy. Part was used to buy two modern cruisers being built for Brazil in British yards, ships that Spanish agents, too, had inquired after. The delays also gave the U.S. Asiatic Squadron under Commodore George Dewey time to assemble along the China coast, take on ammunition and coal, make repairs, and be ready to steam for Manila when the notice of war arrived on April 25. On May 1, just a week after war was declared, a well-prepared Dewey smashed a weaker Spanish fleet in Manila Bay, along with European hopes of imposing an armistice on an embarrassed United States. Had Dewey's first encounter been inconclusive or marked by loss of any U.S. ships, that might not have been the case. The partial caveat to this preparedness rationale for delay, though, is that McKinley, with his seeming humanitarian calculus, never asserted it.

From March's public jeers, when he seemed to stand against the nation's gathering war fever, McKinley's stock soared after May 7, when the news of the U.S. naval triumph arrived from Hong Kong. The public was ecstatic. One chronicler noted, "Manila Bay was hailed as the greatest naval victory in history, and Dewey as the equal of the transcendent Nelson."[19] The president shared in the credit, especially as military success followed military success. The U.S. Army was woefully unprepared to fight overseas, but luckily, not too many Americans had to do so. Most histories mention at least two small battles on land—El Caney and San Juan Hill in Cuba, both on July 1—but the bookends of easy victory were naval: Manila Bay as the opener, then the nearly total destruction of a second Spanish flotilla outside Santiago, Cuba, on July 3.

With the government in Madrid asking for terms by late July, a protocol was signed on August 12 that a peace treaty would be finalized that autumn in Paris. Hostilities were to conclude on the following terms: Spain was to free Cuba and cede Puerto Rico and Guam to the United States, and the United States was to occupy Manila pending the peace treaty's final disposition of the Philippines. No other war declared by the United States has been shorter.

Once the fighting began, McKinley's experience as a wartime staff officer and adjutant made him an unusually competent commander in chief. He took over control of both foreign policy and the direction of the U.S. military, setting up space in the White House, well equipped with telephone and telegraph connections, that became the first presidential "war room." A switchboard with twenty telegraph wires gave McKinley access to French and British cable lines that ran to Cuba and other points in the Caribbean, as well as to U.S. cable lines that connected him to the soldiers in the field. At the peak of the Cuban fighting, the president could exchange messages with the army commander, General William R. Shafter, in twenty minutes.

To determine and implement strategy, McKinley presided over more or less daily meetings that included the secretaries of war and the navy, as well as top officers from both services. Planning for campaigns at sea gave rise to a new Navy Advisory Board. In army matters, McKinley was soon bypassing the current "Commanding General," Nelson A. Miles, whom he thought too much like his nickname, the "peacock." Instead, McKinley made the adjutant general of the army, Henry Corbin, into a de facto army chief of staff.

Nor was the president at all reluctant to directly intervene in military decision making. When General Shafter was slow to embark his troops from Florida to Cuba, McKinley wired, "Sail at once." A mid-June directive to General Miles on troop dispositions was in McKinley's own hand. In July, when Miles recommended acceptance of a Spanish offer to abandon Santiago if they could retain their arms and retreat into the interior, McKinley cabled a blunt refusal: "What you went to Santiago for was the Spanish army. If you allow it to evacuate with its arms, you must meet it somewhere else. This is not war. If the Spanish commander desires to leave the city and its people, let him surrender and then we will discuss the question as to what should be done with them."[20]

Most scholars have given him full credit. Military historian David Healy concluded that "whatever the achievements and blunders of the war effort, there was no question who was in charge. McKinley's admirers and critics alike agreed on his central role, particularly in the troubled affairs of the War Department. Charles G. Dawes, who saw much of McKinley during the war, wrote admiringly: 'The President by his constant watchfulness and supervision of the War Department saved [Secretary of War Russell] Alger from many blunders. His strong hand was always on the helm. . . . If it had not been, the result would have been demoralization.' "[21]

To be sure, some of the painfully long hours the president kept reflected his own ill-advised, politically conventional War and State Department appointments. John Sherman, at seventy-four showing unexpected senility, was too old to be secretary of state. He had been chosen—to his own initial satisfaction—to cap his career with the cabinet's premier post, as well as to open up an Ohio U.S. Senate seat for Mark Hanna. However, his inadequacy became clear as the demands of the State Department burgeoned. He finally resigned on April 25, the day war was declared. Alger, in turn, was a lumber millionaire and state governor who had done good work for the president in Michigan during the 1896 campaign. His appointment was a reward. But he was not an effective war leader, so McKinley took over personal direction of that department, too, until Alger was forced to leave in 1899.

The scandal over "embalmed" wartime beef supplies, for which Alger was somewhat unfairly scapegoated, didn't stick to the administration in political terms. Neither did the loss of 2,500 officers and men from disease—principally typhoid, malaria, and yellow fever—a much higher number than died carrying arms. Indeed, the minimal battlefield losses—27 officers and 318 enlisted dying in combat or from wounds—go far to explain the public memory of what John Hay called "that splendid little war."

Despite the beef scandals and army mismanagement of health conditions, the public was pleased by U.S. military prowess. With so few killed, one historian observed, "[E]ach of the fallen became the focus of wide civic and even statewide homage." When early in the fighting, Ensign Worth Bagley of North Carolina became the one naval officer to be killed by the foe, the funeral was "attended by two thousand soldiers in training and by the whole community

[Raleigh] and hundreds from all over the state, with tributes of flowers from Washington and Annapolis. He was buried with the honors of a brigadier general."[22] Carl Sandburg later recalled that ten thousand people turned out at the train depot when Bagley's Company C returned to Galesburg, Illinois.

Even before the peace protocol with Spain, McKinley used his new popularity and support in Congress to promote his agenda for U.S. expansion. The Senate approved annexation of Hawaii on July 7. August's protocol, while stipulating that Puerto Rico and Guam would be ceded by Spain to the United States and that Cuba would be freed, left Cuba's exact status unclear; that of the Philippines, also torn by internal revolution, remained completely unsettled. Because acquisition of the Philippines has been taken as the beginning of the American empire, McKinley's intentions became a twentieth-century focus.

One 1993 overview, "William McKinley's Enduring Legacy: The Historiographical Debate on the Taking of the Philippine Islands," published by the Naval Institute Press, found a growing consensus that McKinley was "an able president who, particularly after the Battle of Manila Bay, dominated decisions on the islands."[23] Some historians have gone further, imputing a Machiavellian cleverness to his pursuit of imperialism. Others, more restrained, argue that once McKinley knew of the destruction of the Spanish fleet at Manila Bay and quickly took action to increase the ground troops in the Philippines to some 10,000, he may have been reaching a tentative decision to take possession.

Biographers Morgan and Gould, pressing this latter viewpoint, cited the analysis that McKinley himself offered some time later. Letting Spain keep the archipelago would be "cowardly and dishonorable," transferring it to France or Germany would be "bad business," and independence, for which the Filipinos were still unfit, "would soon have anarchy over there worse than Spain's was."[24] These were all sound points. Had McKinley begun to think in May and June about keeping all or most of the Philippines, not just a single island or a naval base, it would have been like the man, Morgan reasoned, to keep that thinking to himself until he could bring the public and the Congress around to that same conclusion.[25] Doubtless his view would not have been set in cement until he saw the public's favorable response to his arguments that autumn.

On October 1, just twenty-three weeks after McKinley had sent his war message to Congress, his peace commissioners began meeting with Spanish counterparts in Paris. No disposition of the Philippines was to be announced until November, minimizing debate in the 1898 midterm elections. In the meantime, McKinley, with Mark Hanna's advice, opted for something unusual: a mid-October presidential campaign tour in six Midwest states.

The one precedent was not auspicious. Andrew Johnson, successor to the assassinated Lincoln, had been the last chief executive to stump the country for the midterm elections of 1866, and the voters repudiated his efforts and themes. Still, McKinley was an elected president, personally popular, the economy was coming out of a long slump, and he had just won a war—added to which, he had a long record as a highly effective speaker.

On October 14, he began a two-week trip involving fifty-seven appearances and major speeches in Omaha, St. Louis, and Chicago. He did not speak for Republican candidates, but talked in a presidential vein about the conduct and motivations of the war and America's need to accept the territories and responsibilities that came with victory and a new world role. For the moment, at least, he had wrapped the Philippine conundrum in the flag and a rekindling national prosperity. "Duty determines destiny," the president said, and this time he was out to lead public opinion toward a redefinition of both.[26]

The response of his beloved Midwest was warm. One newspaper said his return through Indiana and Ohio brought a "continuous ovation," and when the votes were counted on Election Day, the Republicans had held control, losing only nineteen seats in the House and expecting six new U.S. senators from newly chosen state legislatures. The record books showed it was the best midterm result for a post–Civil War Republican administration—a net of only thirteen GOP seats lost versus the closest previous net decline of twenty-one in 1870.

Continuing U.S. warfare in the Philippines, sometimes against the same insurgents who had battled Spain, would be a bone of contention in future elections. Keeping the Philippines, seemingly against the wishes of many inhabitants, fed the negative portraiture of empire. What would not become a domestic political issue until 1914–16, although they reshaped global geopolitics, were two new emerging polarities and one new entente: the crystallizing rivalries between Britain and Germany and between the United States and Japan, and the reemerging collaboration of the English-speaking peoples.

THE EMERGING ANGLO-AMERICAN ENTENTE

The forebears of William McKinley, Henry Cabot Lodge, and Theodore Roosevelt were, respectively, Scots-Irish and English, largely English, and Dutch-English. But each man went through an intriguing evolution in his attitude toward ancestral Britain: prickly sensitivity and anger at perceived inattention or commercial injury in the 1870s and 1880s gave way to cousinship and incipient alliance in the 1890s as the American place in the world climbed toward Britain's.

Both stages had their logic. In the 1870s and 1880s, upper-class Northerners like Lodge and Roosevelt had been miffed by British ignorance of the United States and condescension toward it, especially by high Tories. McKinley, attuned to labor and commerce, resented what he saw as using the United States as a dumping ground for cheaper British manufactures made possible by Britain's lower wages, bigger factories, greater economy of scale, and access to raw materials. Absent protective tariffs, McKinley argued in the 1870s and 1880s, British manufactured goods would overpower fledgling U.S. industries and erode America's much higher wage levels.

By the late 1890s, America's expanding navy, soaring fortunes, ballooning manufacturing industries, and booming exports were building confidence in all three men, even if TR and Cabot Lodge grumbled about America's upper classes being full of jumped-up usurers and linoleum makers. British aristocrats had been marrying U.S. heiresses in ever-larger numbers, while Londoners were coming to rely on ingenious Americans for their electrical industry and for the construction of their "tube," or subway. U.S. export capacity now scared the British as opposed to the reverse situation in 1850 or 1870. A British writer, W. T. Stead, found "the Americanization of the world" to be well under way. Even the British Admiralty was starting to contemplate its own reluctant nuptials: Royal Navy supremacy in European, African, and Asian waters would be wed to U.S. Navy dominance in the Western Hemisphere.

In the eighties, the Democratic party under Cleveland was the one preferred by the British elites. One British minister to the United States, Sir Lionel Sackville-West, had to return home after writing a foolish letter, which became public, recommending a vote for Cleveland. Upper-class Britain favored free trade, opposed U.S. tariffs, and disliked the industrial plutocracy, and for that matter had disproportionately supported the cavalier-seeming Democratic South in the Civil War. The politics of the Protestant British immigrant population in the United States, however, was quite different.

Taken together, English, Scottish, Welsh, and Scots-Irish immigrants in the United States circa 1890 were almost as numerous as the Germans or Catholic Irish. Overall, they were more Republican than any native-born Protestant American stock save greater New England Yankees. In a few industrial locales, the Protestant British-born population—mechanics, miners, engineers, managers, and shop foremen—outnumbered the other immigrant groups. Most were pillars of the tariff system, knowing that it sustained pay scales 50 or even 100 percent higher than those of their brothers and cousins in Britain.

McKinley's section of northeastern Ohio was particularly full of British Republicans. Some were Welsh coal miners and foremen who called the GOP *plaid werinol*, Welsh for the party of the people. Others were English wheat farmers and sheep raisers who had flocked to this part of Ohio after Britain's repeal of agricultural protection in the 1840s. In 1893, six hundred kilted Scottish steelworkers marched in a large McKinley parade in Akron. Columbiana County, on the eastern edge of McKinley's old congressional district, was the center of the U.S. clay and ceramics industry, run and substantially manned by thousands of immigrants from the similar potteries of England's West Midlands.

Under McKinley, and with the help of American imperialists like Lodge, TR, and Admiral A. T. Mahan and Anglophiles like John Hay, secretary of state from 1898 to 1905, the Republicans quietly became the more British-connected party. It also helped that Bryan and the Democrats, in their Populist incarnation, had attacked British finance as the evil senior partner of Wall Street.

As war clouds thickened in 1898, British support for the United States against Spain was so obvious that the Madrid government briefly strengthened its fortifications on the border with Gibraltar. McKinley, in turn, was pro-British from his first months in office. He supported—without success—a far-reaching arbitration treaty before the U.S. Senate in 1897 by which Britain and the United States promised to submit their differences to such resolution. He relied on Britain in 1898 for covert assistance during the war months and reciprocated by muting U.S. sentiment against Britain in the 1899–1901 Boer War (McKinley had to squelch a pro-Boer plank in the 1900 GOP platform). Through John Hay, McKinley worked closely with London regarding China and the Boxer Rebellion, evolving the Open Door policy (1900), which sought to maintain Chinese territorial integrity while opening the Chinese empire to "equal and impartial trade" with all powers.

To cement the informal alliance taking shape, the British also worked out satisfactory conclusions on two other matters: resolution of the controversial boundary between Alaska and Canada (1903) and replacement of the old Clayton-Bulwer Treaty with the new Hay-Pauncefote Treaty (1901), giving British blessings to the U.S. construction and fortification of a Panama Canal. Both were signed under Theodore Roosevelt but set in motion under McKinley.

The spurs to entente included shared ancestry and the rising reference to that bond in both nations. Besides which, the no-longer-vexing North American frontier squabbles had given way to an embryonic sense of shared Anglo-Saxon globalism. The biggest factor, though, involved the new roles and rivalries creeping onto the world stage.

Several historians have argued that the Anglo-American goodwill surrounding the war was too transient to mark a watershed. Although true as stated—by 1900, the Boer War did pour some cold water over earlier mutual enthusiasm—overemphasis on one particular clump of trees loses sight of the changing geopolitical forest. If the Spanish-American War made one thing clear to British diplomats and military theorists, it was the awesome strength that the United States could be expected to deploy as its global military and commercial objectives matured. In the words of Lord Bryce, "[T]he Republic is as wealthy as any two of the greatest European nations, and is capable, if she chooses, of quickly calling into being a vast fleet and a vast army. Her wealth and power has in it something almost alarming."[27]

Stewart Woodford, the U.S. minister to Spain in 1898, reported how stunned the Spanish had been to see the U.S. Congress vote $50 million more for unspecified defense out of unneeded treasury funds. The odd stickler for absolute naval supremacy aside, British leaders saw more pluses than minuses. In 1890, the U.S. Navy had ranked twelfth internationally, behind China and Turkey. By 1900, the United States was sixth, with shipbuilding rising apace; and in 1906, *Jane's Fighting Ships* for the first time actually placed the U.S. Navy second to the British.[28] Britain's naval edge might be at risk in a contest with Germany, but the combined naval supremacy of the English-speaking powers was safe and climbing.

Moreover, just as turn-of-the-century Anglo-German relations were souring, the United States, too, became increasingly suspicious of the kaiser's new ambitions in the Pacific and Caribbean. First whetted in the 1880s in Samoa, Washington's displeasure was aroused again in 1895 by German attempts to secure a coaling station in Haiti, coupled with reports of Berlin's interest in buying Cuba from Spain. War with Spain in 1898 brought these tensions to new heights.

By July 1898, a month after Dewey had beaten Spain's Asian squadron, the German navy had sent six ships to Manila Bay, including a troop transport with fourteen hundred men. Told that command of Far Eastern waters would pass to the power controlling the Philippines, the kaiser's government had its eye on the Sulu Archipelago, the southern Philippine island of Mindanao, the Carolines, and all of the Samoan group. At first, the German ships outgunned Dewey's squadron, and, according to one naval observer, "acted as if Manila Bay were absolutely in their possession." They also kept in close touch with Spanish authorities, who openly expected the German flotilla to come to their aid.[29] Dewey thought he might have to fight the Germans and requested reinforcements before U.S.-Spanish peace terms were resolved. These were sent, and German belligerence eased, albeit Berlin made clear its desire for whatever territory the Americans left to the Spanish in the Philippines and vicinity.

In September, Germany and Spain reached a secret understanding that Berlin would get the Caroline and Ladrone (Marianas) Islands. When Spain's Far Eastern divestiture was finalized in December, the kaiser wound up with the Marianas (less Guam, taken by the United States), the Carolines, and the Palaus, with Germany having already bought the Marshalls in 1895, and the new acquisitions completed an island chain that reached fifteen hundred miles from the Bismarck Archipelago to the Marianas.

German activity in the Caribbean also increased. When the kaiser's government used gunboat diplomacy against Haiti in November 1897, a U.S. senior naval officer sent to investigate German penetration predicted that "before many years have passed, Germany will succeed in acquiring one or more territorial possessions in the Western Hemisphere."[30] The next U.S. concern, over possible German interference in an independent Cuba, led in January 1901 to the congressionally drawn Platt Amendment, which Cuba's constitutional convention was required to accept that spring. Cuba undertook not to impair its independence through a treaty with a foreign power, specifying that the United States could intervene "for the preservation of Cuban independence and the maintenance of stable government."[31]

American concern about Japan also intensified during the late 1890s, first over Hawaii and then over the Philippines. The insistence in the 1896 Republican platform that the United States should control Hawaii and exclude foreign interference prompted McKinley's quick request for annexation in 1897. That spring, the Senate Foreign Relations Committee's own concurring report likewise identified strategic considerations as "the main argument in favor." According to the senators, "The issue in Hawaii is not between monarchy and the Republic. . . . The issue is whether, in that inevitable struggle, Asia [i.e., Japan] or America shall have the vantage ground of the naval 'key of the Pacific,' the commercial 'Cross-roads of the Pacific.'"[32]

Because of an influx of agricultural laborers, Hawaii's Japanese population was already one quarter of the islands' total, outnumbering Americans by more than three to one. When the Hawaiian government refused in March 1897 to admit more Japanese, Tokyo sent a warship, the cruiser *Namiwa*, while senior officials hinted at even stronger action. The McKinley administration, even while pursuing Hawaiian annexation, drafted a possible war plan against Japan and sent three U.S. warships to Honolulu. In June, naval authorities instructed the local U.S. commander that if the Japanese invaded, he should "land a suitable force and announce officially provisional assumption of protectorate pending a treaty of annexation."[33] As the Senate could not mobilize a two-thirds majority for an annexation treaty, the president told Massachusetts Senator George Hoar that "if something [annexation] be not done, there will be before long another Revolution, and Japan will get control." However, in December, the Japanese backed off and began turning their attention in the Pacific elsewhere—to the Philippines.

When the battle of Manila Bay was fought, two Japanese warships were also visiting, and after Dewey's victory suggested Spain's local rule was near its end, Japan officially offered to oversee the Philippines if the United States declined to take up that role.[34] After the Spanish departure when Filipino rebels under Emilio Aguinaldo kept fighting against the United States, it was Tokyo that Aguinaldo pressed hardest for recognition of his revolutionary regime.[35]

Not just expansion, then, but global geopolitics underpinned the desire of both nations, Britain and the United States, for close relations as the twentieth century unfolded. Henry Adams surmised that "The sudden appearance of Germany is the grizzly terror which in twenty years . . . frightened England into America's arms."[36] In the United States, meanwhile, Admiral Dewey could declare by 1899 that America's next war would be with Germany. And by 1902 and 1903, after Germany's part in a coercion of Venezuela, the British ambassador in Washington reported to Whitehall that "suspicion of the German emperor's designs in the Caribbean sea is shared by the Administration, the press and the public alike."[37] To complete the triangle, John Hay wrote to Senator Lodge from London that "the jealousy and animosity felt toward us in Germany is something which can scarcely be exaggerated. . . . The *Vaterland* is all on fire with greed and terror of us."[38]

Few histories of the Spanish-American War give this larger context the attention it deserves. But, in short, the decisive geopolitics of the first half of the twentieth century—that Britain and the United States as allies would defeat Germany and Japan—took a critical leap forward under McKinley.

MCKINLEY AS A PIVOTAL FOREIGN POLICY PRESIDENT

The evidence for this judgment ranges from his skilled wartime leadership and institutional innovations to his successful exertion on behalf of U.S. trade expansion and reciprocity, international arbitration, Anglo-American entente, the enablement of the Panama Canal, and the U.S. emergence as a two-ocean naval and military power. McKinley, more than anyone else in Washington from 1897 to 1901, managed and promoted the transformation of the United States from the still internally preoccupied and globally uninvolved nation of the early 1890s to the world power of the 1900s.

Because his first cabinet officers for the State and War Departments, Sherman and Alger, were political choices born of the older, more parochial nineteenth-century United States and its relaxed priorities, the president himself had to take over much of the leadership of these departments as global tensions deepened in late 1897 and 1898. In crisis terms, it may have been the making of him. By the time that Woodrow Wilson, who voted for McKinley over Bryan, published the fifteenth edition of *Congressional Government* in 1900, his preface acknowledged the transformation brought about by McKinley:

When foreign affairs play a prominent part in the politics and policy of a nation, its Executive must of necessity be its guide; must utter every initial, take every first step of action, supply the information on which it is to act, suggest and in large measure control its conduct. The President of the United States is now, as of course, at the front of affairs, as no president, except Lincoln, has been since the first quarter of the nineteenth century.[39]

Not only did he fill both departmental roles with considerable skill during the transition before he could identify successors, but his choices were men who were to win kudos, John Hay and Elihu Root. To them, he handed over departmental, although not overall, decision making. In a memorial address in 1902, Hay had this to say of the man he served:

> In dealing with foreign powers he will take rank with the greatest of our diplomatists. It was a world of which he had little special knowledge before coming to the presidency. But his marvellous adaptability was in nothing more remarkable than in the firm grasp he immediately displayed in international relations. In preparing for war and in the restoration of peace he was alike adroit, courteous and far-sighted.[40]

Both Hay and Root became pillars of the GOP foreign policy establishment, as did other McKinley appointees who went on to become president or vice president: Theodore Roosevelt, William Howard Taft, Charles G. Dawes, and Charles Fairbanks. One can argue, reasonably, that McKinley identified and advanced a considerable part of the high-level Republican talent pool for the 1896–1932 period in which the GOP generally governed. Roosevelt, Taft, Dawes, Fairbanks, Hay, and Root all lived longer than the man who advanced or appointed them, and they left many favorable comments on McKinley and hardly any that were otherwise. They all knew who made the major decisions, and it was one of his unique attributes not only not to hog the credit or limelight, but to let his subordinates have their share and sometimes more. Personal public relations was neither his skill nor his preoccupation.

It is now time to turn to a related argument: that McKinley was not merely the political architect of the realignment of 1896 and America's new world role, but the senior coarchitect of much of the modernism and reformism, domestic and international, that is too often thought to have begun with Theodore Roosevelt.

5

Political Success,
Domestic Progress, and the
McKinley-Roosevelt Continuum

The combination of the "Democratic Depression" of 1893 and severe ethno-cultural hostilities between new immigrant workers and old-stock agrarians created an urban revulsion against the Democrats which lasted into the late 1920s. . . . The essentially nostalgic and colonial character of the [Bryan] insurgents' appeal produced a violently sectional reaction throughout the metropole; the Democratic party in that region sank into an impotence which, save for a limited upswing between 1910 and 1916, lasted for a generation.
                    Walter Dean Burnham, *The American Party Systems*

The implication to be drawn from Professor Burnham, an expert on American political realignment, is that electoral upheaval explains more of William McKinley's extraordinary domestic policy success than any tabulation of mere legislative enactment. Through shrewd politicking at a critical juncture, McKinley ensured that the economy and society of the early-twentieth-century United States would have a modern industrial and urban bias, supported by an increasingly strong presidency and by a no longer stalemated party system able to marginalize agrarian protest.

Of the six or seven national party realignments in U.S. electoral history, most have intertwined with an important policy watershed, giving their presidential architect a leg up on great or near-great status. Viewed through this lens, McKinley's interrelated successes—a new period of economic prosperity, including the entrenchment of the protective tariff framework in 1897 and the gold standard in

1900—ended a quarter century of bitter acrimony over currency, money supply, and tariffs with a clear decision in favor of manufacturing, global commerce, and a sound currency *with* mild inflation.

True, the gold standard and high tariffs, wearing out their welcome, would both need to be replaced at the end of the industrial Republican cycle in 1932, which is another story (and another realignment). But it must be pointed out that McKinley, the currency straddle bug and trade reciprocity advocate, was more flexible on both issues than the business-establishment Republican presidents to follow in the 1920s. His second term, of which he served only six months, would have basked in a brightening ideological sun, encouraging his Lincolnian streak on subjects ranging from tax fairness to attempts to reduce trusts and monopolies, especially those nurtured by special-interest tariff provisions.

Alas, because the Ohioan's modus operandi was to keep his own counsel, write down very little, and let others think that they were doing much of the steering, he did not leave the sort of paper trail usually required to pique the interest of intellectuals. Unrecorded presidential conversations with admiring reformers and progressives were just that: *unrecorded*. In historical terms he could not have imagined, the bullets that eliminated his second-term tenure from September 1901 through March 1905 contributed to his great reputational loss and Theodore Roosevelt's gain. The Progressive era is said to begin with TR, when in fact McKinley put in place the political organization, the antimachine spirit, the critical party realignment, the cadre of skilled GOP statesmen who spanned a quarter of a century, the expert inquiries, the firm commitment to popular and economic democracy, and the leadership needed from 1896 through 1901 when TR was still maturing.

McKinley, fifteen years older than the man he took as vice president in 1900, was a man who achieved much, portions of it far-reaching, by avoiding the limelight and building a reputation, popularity, and gravitas that ultimately allowed him to face down the Senate hierarchs and Eastern machine leaders and win the 1896 Republican presidential nomination virtually unencumbered. TR could never have done that; even in the years 1897–98, when, almost forty years old and assistant secretary of the navy, he appeared to many who dealt with him as headstrong and immature.

His later progressivism was still half-submerged in an upper-class derogation of labor unions and routine insistence on a gold currency. Roosevelt did not back McKinley for the nomination in 1896, unlike Robert La Follette, Lincoln Steffens, and others later famous as Progressives. Instead, be supported Reed, the Maine conservative.

What Roosevelt had was independence, intellectual curiosity, and dash. His decision to leave the Navy Department to fight in Cuba as lieutenant colonel of the First U.S. Volunteer Cavalry—the famous (because he made them so) Rough Riders—bespoke the shrewd political instinct intertwined with his impetuosity. Along with Admiral Dewey, TR became one of the two public heroes of the Spanish-American War, such being a proven national political elevator.[1] Upon TR's return, Thomas Platt, the same boss at odds with McKinley, promptly enlisted the hero of San Juan Hill as the 1898 candidate to hold his machine's vital but endangered patronage bastion: the New York governorship. Although Roosevelt won only narrowly, a year and a half later he had become the grassroots GOP choice to replace Vice President Garret Hobart, whose death had opened up second place on the 1900 national ticket.

Beyond amplifying the domestic successes interwoven with McKinley's realignment of party politics, this chapter also reinterprets the respective roles of McKinley and Roosevelt in bringing progressivism and reform to a head in the new century. The two administrations must be taken together, with McKinley being the essential foundation builder and the former Rough Rider the greater attention getter and crusader.

POLITICAL REALIGNMENT AND DOMESTIC POLICY SUCCESS

Political scientists explaining McKinley's role as a realignment president usually give him domestic laurels. Just in itself, the election of 1896 resolved a long economic debate, empowered Republican policy priorities, and dovetailed with a revival of prosperity. Here is one historian's explanation:

> Party leaders contended over alternative explanations for the depression of 1893 and the ensuing economic crisis, and

Bryan and McKinley each sought to persuade voters that he had the correct explanation for the cause of the depression as well as the most effective cure. Each tried to mobilize voters around explanatory ideological positions with which those voters could identify. In the end, McKinley's explanation in terms of the tariff made sense to discontented urban-industrial workingmen.[2]

According to a sampling of Democratic and Republican newspapers in the Midwest, the change in the two parties' credibility between 1892 and 1894 previewed the 1896 outcome. Protection won. Democratic journals that had strongly indicted Republican tariffs in 1892 were massively backtracking two years later. As the Republicans attacked "Democratic hard times" and characterized the tariff as Republican "wage protection," two-thirds of the Democratic papers said that the tariff issue was now settled, which would restore good times.[3]

If neither explanation of the downturn—too little silver in monetary use versus a business contraction triggered by manufacturers' fears of tariff reduction—seems sufficient, most voters had broader reasons for their 1896 decisions. Through McKinley's candidacy, tariff protection enlarged its appeal to urban and industrial voters with sound money, proven commitment to labor, and ethnic and religious ecumenicalism rather than evangelism. The long-term GOP empowerment in 1896, according to Burnham, came from the economic and cultural shifts in the two parties' national coalitions and agendas:

> Essentially, the reorganization of the Democratic Party during the Bryan era made it to a very large degree the vehicle of colonial, periphery-oriented dissent against the industrial metropole-center. It was also the vehicle through which the myriad [largely rural] island communities surviving from the nineteenth century sought on occasion to ward off absorption into the larger society being brought into existence under the auspices of industrial capitalism.[4]

Another historian, Paul Kleppner, saw in "the party of McKinley" a new Republican majority "quite different socially from that which the party had mobilized in the 1850s. This was not the party of evangelical Protestantism, not the 'party of piety,' but the 'party of prosperity.'"[5] McKinley even carried Southern and border-state cities where Republican support had been inconsequential to non-existent in Lincoln's day.

A Republican pamphleteer, out to condense McKinley's four-year record into a 1900 reelection slogan, might have chosen "Prosperity, Protection, and Progress." The economy turned up in 1897 and pretty much kept rising through 1902, save for a very mild contraction between late 1899 and late 1900. Prosperity had a new base in place. According to economist Milton Friedman, during this 1897 to 1902 rebound, the U.S. money supply rose some 80 percent, largely brought about by booming new gold production in Australia, South Africa, and the Yukon. Per capita output, in turn, rose by an average 4 ½ percent a year.[6]

To most industrial workers, McKinley's "full dinner pail" promise became a reality. Barns in Kansas and Nebraska, a visitor reported, had a new coat of paint. Stock market indexes, celebratory verging on euphoric, showed a rise of some 70 percent between August 1896 and August 1899.[7] It was, in short, the seeming Republican boom after the seeming Democratic bust (the reverse would end the industrial Republican era when the GOP crash of 1929 to 1933 led into the Democratic boom and realignment of the 1930s).

With hard times fading as an election issue, the "party of prosperity" enjoyed the fruits—McKinley's national victory margin rose from 596,000 in 1896 to 860,000 in 1900, and the Republicans also held the House and Senate in both midterm elections, 1898 and 1902. The break with the quarter century of stalemate from 1874 to 1896 was complete.

As a domestic political and economic success story, this one was not far behind Franklin D. Roosevelt and the New Deal comeback from depression. Hallmarks included the two great issues effectively resolved. On the currency front, McKinley had begun a major attempt in early 1897, with the economy still weak, to secure an international agreement for a bimetallic system using both gold and silver in a new value ratio. The French were favorable, provided Germany and especially Britain also agreed. At first, the latter had mild interest, according to McKinley biographer Lewis Gould, because of the possible benefit of renewed silver coinage to British India. Also, some in the British government liked how renewed bimetallism might guarantee defeat for the anti-British Bryan in any second presidential race.[8]

Through the summer, accord seemed possible. The Bank of England announced that upon agreement being reached, it would hold one-fifth of its note value in silver. This, not surprisingly, aroused gold standard forces in the United States, and when the government of India also protested to London about the silver plan's risk, the scheme died.

Politically, McKinley had kept the promise in his inaugural address of "constant endeavor to secure it [bimetallism] by cooperation with the other great commercial powers of the world."[9] Practically, however, the rising production of gold and the mushrooming of the U.S. money supply made it obvious by 1899 that further monetization of silver was unnecessary. Plentiful gold had achieved what mild inflationists wanted from silver. In 1900 the White House proposed and Congress enacted the Gold Standard Act, declaring the gold dollar to be the standard unit of value and providing that greenbacks and Treasury notes alike "shall be redeemed in gold coin."[10] Such was the ebb of the currency debate that Nebraska, South Dakota, Wyoming, Utah, and Washington switched to McKinley in the 1900 election, leaving Bryan, in his second race, only four faithful Western states: Colorado, Montana, Idaho, and Nevada, the hard core of silver production and sentiment.

On the tariff front, the Dingley Act of 1897, like the McKinley Tariff seven years earlier, was flawed by the hundreds of rate increases and special provisions tacked on by the time of the House-Senate conference. House Ways and Means Committee Chairman Nelson Dingley, a McKinley friend and ally, had planned to drop many rates below 1890 levels, but the lobbies prevailed.[11] Even so, because the tariff mismanagement collapsed that issue for Democrats in 1894, the Dingley Act had little effect in the 1898 or 1900 elections. The rates controversy was not over, but according to one analysis, "for McKinley, the specific rates in the Dingley Act were less important than the possibility for negotiating reductions in the future, which the reciprocity clauses offered."[12]

As chapter 2 has discussed, between 1881 and 1890, McKinley supported a series of reforms including the use of a federal tariff commission to adjust rates on a more scientific basis, an overhaul of customs collection, and the earliest provision for tariff reciprocity. Within six months of becoming president, he was again immersed, recruiting Iowan John A. Kasson to head a newly established reciprocity bureau in the State Department. Part of the imperative came from the huge growth in U.S. trade, especially exports, during the late 1890s. U.S. industry had ballooned, passing Britain in manufacturing capacity. Now the need was to keep expanding exports. Failure to do so, McKinley thought, would mean industrial overproduction, insufficient demand, and an economic downturn.

The explosive growth of U.S. trade had already trampled earlier free-trade warnings about protection building fatal economic walls. Between 1865 and 1900, U.S. merchandise exports had quintupled from $261 million to $1.53 billion, with the fastest growth coming in manufactures (now 35 percent of total)—mostly metals, machinery, and transport equipment. In all of these, U.S. companies were becoming world leaders. During the low tariff era between 1846 and 1861, imports and exports had been roughly equal in value. However, by 1897 and 1898, as prosperity returned under high tariff protection, merchandise exports surged far beyond imports. In 1897, the surplus was $286 million, in 1898 a staggering $616 million. By 1899, the United States was exporting almost twice as much merchandise as came in, utterly unprecedented.

On one hand, this was a triumph—Republicans reasonably boasted about tariffs' effectiveness in nurturing such successful industries. Yet it was also a caution: selling so much abroad would be hard to sustain without taking more foreign goods in return, thus the need to shift from pure protection to an emphasis on reciprocity and bargaining.

The chief of the federal Bureau of Foreign Commerce, in a magazine article, found it "almost incredible that we should be sending cutlery to Sheffield, pig iron to Birmingham, silks to France, watch cases to Switzerland . . . or building sixty locomotives for British railroads."[13] True enough, but the extraordinary progress in science, invention, and industry in the United States from the Civil War to 1900 was on a scale with what Britain had achieved from 1760 to

1830 during the gathering of the Industrial Revolution. The great
technological exhibitions of early Victorian Britain had stunned the
world, and so did the displays in the technology-filled American
Pavilion of the Paris Exposition in 1900 and the U.S. Pan-American
Exposition in 1901.

Since 1890, McKinley had been urging trade reciprocity as a
corollary of protection. In 1901, his intention to frame it as a
coequal principle was already raising warning flags among staunch
protectionists. The president planned his major address for the Pan-
American Exposition in September—he told Dawes that "it will be
the most important one of my life"—because much of the negotiated reciprocity involved Latin America.[14] His great emphasis
would also send a message to the new Congress convening in
December.

In McKinley's view, tariffs were enough of an engine of the U.S.
economy to serve, when reconnected to pistons of reciprocity
rather than simple protection, as drivers of wide-ranging change. In
negotiations with the French over possible bimetallism, he had held
out a carrot of tariff concessions under the new reciprocity provisions. In 1901, after the giant U.S. Steel combination was formed,
one GOP congressman from Wisconsin introduced a bill to reduce
tariff rates on steel products that competed with those of the new
Goliath.[15] It was a tactic that the president himself had pursued.
The McKinley Tariff of 1890 had slapped at the Democratic-linked
sugar (refining) trust by putting imported sugar on the free list.[16] As
trusts and combinations proliferated like rabbits in the late 1890s,
high-priced products of monopolies became logical possibilities for
tariff concessions under reciprocity. With respect to wealth and
income distribution, reciprocal tariff reductions could also be used
to redistribute economic burdens assuming lost tariff dollars could
be replaced from a new income or inheritance tax.

Despite momentum for international reciprocity in 1898 and
1899, Senate inaction blocked the multiple agreements the president submitted. His lopsided reelection, however, suggested a new
balance of power in Washington. During the summer of 1901,
according to White House Secretary Cortelyou, McKinley prepared "for a series of speeches in which he proposed to develop
progressively his ideas on the extension of our foreign trade

through the means of reciprocity treaties." He also asked for "the collection of data on the subject of trusts." Cortelyou later recalled, "I never saw him more determined on anything than on this."[17] Senator Henry Cabot Lodge told Rhode Island's Nelson Aldrich that not only would reciprocity be pressed in the upcoming Congress, but that proreciprocity majorities were likely to emerge in the Senate Foreign Relations Committee unless protectionist senators rallied their colleagues to oppose the White House.[18]

At home, McKinley was also anxious to reunite a nation still divided, North and South, by Civil War memory—and, East and West, by a quarter century of gold versus silver conflict. His international negotiations for bimetallism made strides in winning back the silverite West. This started in the 1898 midterms, when the GOP gained congressional seats in California, Kansas, South Dakota, Washington, and Wyoming. Then, in the 1900 election, vice presidential nominee Roosevelt successfully stumped the sagebrush states where he had ranched and hunted in the 1880s and recruited his volunteer cavalry in 1898.

Ecumenicalism, arbitration, and outreach, in turn, were almost extensions of McKinley's personality. He had applied them to labor, Catholics, and Democrats in Ohio, and as president, he reached out to the South as well as the silver states. Democrat Grover Cleveland, who had hired a substitute rather than fight in the Civil War, later stirred a furor in 1887 by ordering the return to the South of captured battle flags. As a Northern veteran, McKinley could extend the olive branch with near impunity.

When the Spanish-American War started, McKinley recommissioned two former Confederate brigadiers, Fitzhugh Lee and "Fighting Joe" Wheeler, as "a symbol that the old days are gone." For months, Dixie leaders had been saying that Southerners would flock to the colors in numbers that would submerge and replace memories of the 1861–65 strife, and McKinley's actions were warmly applauded below the Mason-Dixon Line. By one account, "these appointments and the enlistments of many other Southerners brought a unity the country had not seen since the end of the Civil War. Now, instead of singing 'Dixie' or 'Marching Through Georgia,' the country was singing 'He Laid Away a Suit of Gray to Wear the Union Blue.'"[19]

Mawkish middle-class sentiment, to be sure. But taken together, these successes—in politics, prosperity, finance, technological progress, and national reunification—helped to make McKinley the most popular president since Lincoln.

MCKINLEY, ROOSEVELT, AND REFORM, 1896 TO 1904

Theodore Roosevelt, on becoming president, knew the depth of public affection for his slain predecessor. Nevertheless, his statement in September 1901 that "in this hour of deep and terrible bereavement . . . it shall be my aim to continue absolutely unbroken the policy of President McKinley" had a downside, given the dead president's unique leadership style. TR bound himself to extend the sort of policy making that McKinley's 1897 to 1901 record *appeared* to represent, which is to say a mostly conventional conservatism.

TR charging off in pursuit of his own political initiatives would have gone down poorly, of course. Even so, the result was to hamstring Roosevelt in pursuing the ideological changes that McKinley had up his carefully guarded sleeve but which, for tactical reasons, he had not put on the proverbial table. Tariff reciprocity, reasonably publicized, was an exception; TR just didn't have the expertise or Capitol Hill support to lead that battle. Perversely, the constraint of Roosevelt's first thirty-eight months in turn reflected back on McKinley, appearing to confirm that it was his dullness that a restive TR was obliged to extend.

Some chronology will indicate otherwise. In 1896, TR had been much more of a conservative Republican than McKinley. He supported the machine favorite for the presidential nomination, House Speaker Reed. He was a gold currency man with no Midwestern ifs, ands, or buts. He disliked labor unions and Grangers. Where McKinley shared some of Bryan's suspicions of the East and was careful in derogating his Democratic rival, TR voiced the sort of arrogance heard in Manhattan or Boston clubs, worrying about "a red government of lawlessness and dishonesty as phantastic and vicious as the Paris Commune itself."[20] His reformism was mostly of the mugwump sort, emphasizing the civil service and municipal corruption.

The views of the two men converged somewhat after Roosevelt won the New York governorship in 1898. Silver-gold divisions were falling by the wayside; TR's tariff positions moved farther from the free-trade theology he had heard at Harvard and closer to standard Republican thinking. Governing in New York also required him to confront two subjects that McKinley had earlier faced in Ohio: labor reform and tax fairness.

Roosevelt devoted fully one-fifth of his first annual message to issues affecting workingmen, a sign that he was broadening his base. During his two years in Albany, he proposed and the legislature passed measures to add factory inspectors, enforce the eight-hour day for state workers, increase protection for women and children in factories, inspect tenements used for manufacturing, and limit drug clerks' hours. However, Platt and the legislators rejected his most advanced labor proposal, an employers' liability bill.

As for tax fairness, Roosevelt got drawn into the legislature's attempt to redefine taxable real estate to include the franchised use of city streets by utility and transportation companies. Even when compromise legislation stalled in the courts, the ruckus spotlighted a key issue: relative tax burdens. TR also proposed a novel approach to curbing the trusts: the use of government to publicize information on companies' assets, debts, and profits. Mild state legislation in this vein was enacted in 1899. In December 1901, Roosevelt as president made a similar proposal for federal-level publicity (this while judicial implementation of the Sherman Antitrust Act remained uncertain).

McKinley's influence had quietly secured much farther reaching labor and tax legislation in Ohio. However, the two men's methods represented different eras and psychologies. McKinley avoided rhetoric in favor of strategic enlistment and backstairs orchestration; Roosevelt anticipated the Progressive era climate by jousting with epithets and accusations as much as legislation. He infuriated the state GOP machine and its business allies with blunt comments— desiring, for example, to crack down on corporations "organized in a spirit of mere greed, for improper speculative purposes" and holding that "the man who by swindling or wrongdoing acquires great wealth for himself at the expense of his fellow, stands as low morally as any predatory medieval nobleman."[21]

In 1900, TR decided not to reappoint state insurance Commissioner Louis F. Payn, an organization stalwart who had taken an improper half-million-dollar loan from an insurance-connected bank. Despite his compromise with the machine on a replacement, the sum of Roosevelt's provocations had become unacceptable. Platt announced in April that the governor "will not be renominated for his present office."

Vice President Hobart's death, however, had opened up a new avenue: obtaining Roosevelt's selection as McKinley's new running mate. There were two problems. First, Roosevelt said he didn't want to run for vice president but again for governor, and most of the time he seemed to mean it. As a gentleman historian, TR knew that aside from the vice presidents who succeeded Lincoln and Garfield, from 1860 to 1896, the office was a ticket to nowhere. Hannibal Hamlin, Schuyler Colfax, Henry Wilson, William Wheeler, Thomas Hendricks, Levi Morton, and Adlai Stevenson each served their four years without creating any demand for their advancement. Friends' advice about a changing vice presidential role rang hollow.

Problem number two was that the president didn't care for Tom Platt and hadn't for a long time. In 1888, deal-seeking emissaries from Platt had provoked McKinley to rare "violent profanity."[22] Why would a president who had refused to deal with Platt in 1888 or as a nomination seeker in 1896 now be willing to let the New Yorker appear to impose a vice presidential nominee on his triumphant reelection? Small wonder that TR was ambiguous about what he wanted (or want he wanted to say he wanted).

Hobart, who had become the president's friend, sometimes served as his eyes and ears in the Senate. McKinley's first choice to replace him was Iowa Senator William B. Allison, a smooth operator who could have helped as a backstairs White House liaison with the ever-troublesome upper house. But Allison had no interest. Other possibilities included Congressman Jonathan Dolliver of Iowa and Navy Secretary John Long. Mark Hanna, with whom McKinley was not so close as before, vehemently opposed taking the volatile Roosevelt. Because Hanna had some thoughts of succeeding McKinley himself in 1904, he might not have been entirely disinterested.

McKinley would have noted something else. In 1896, he had prided himself on being the candidate of "The People Against the Bosses." By the time the 1900 convention started, the New York governor was just as obviously the people's choice. His bent even resembled McKinley's. The *New York Times* observed that TR had "torn down the curtain that shut in the Governor and taken the public into his confidence . . . beyond what was ever known before."[23] In some conversations with Henry Cabot Lodge and others, McKinley showed interest in taking TR on the ticket.[24] What could not be accepted was any appearance of dictation by Platt and his usual ally, Pennsylvania machine leader Quay.

Indeed, that year the McKinley administration had been quietly at work helping to weaken or replace old-line state machines and leaders, most notably in Illinois, Iowa, and Wisconsin in the Midwest, but also in New Jersey. Roosevelt running again in New York, beating and even terminating the Platt organization, would have been their first choice. Charles Dawes was the presidential adviser who tended party upheavals in the Midwest—defeating a machine resurgence in Illinois and supporting the takeovers of Progressives (and 1896 McKinley lieutenants) Robert La Follette in Wisconsin and Albert B. Cummins in Iowa. Officially, he was the federal comptroller of the currency; unofficially, he was close to McKinley in the same son-figure way that McKinley had been to Rutherford Hayes.

While Hanna was readying a last-minute convention attempt to stop Roosevelt's nomination and complaining that the White House wouldn't act, Dawes set up a telephone call to McKinley's chief secretary George Cortelyou, with the president listening in on another telephone. Dawes described to them how an enraged Hanna wanted to block a Quay-orchestrated stampede to Roosevelt with a White House–backed countermove for Secretary Long. Dawes told Cortelyou and the president that any such Hanna effort would boomerang.[25] As Dawes later described the event in his journal, he then took dictation of a "hands-off" presidential message to Hanna:

The President's close friend must not undertake to commit
the Administration to any candidate. It has no candidate. The
Convention must make the nomination. The Administration
would not if it could. . . . The Administration wants the
choice of the Convention and the President's friend must not
dictate to the Convention.[26]

Hanna acquiesced, and Dawes conveyed word back to the president. The next day, Dawes went back to Washington and spent four
hours talking politics with McKinley.[27] A week later, Dawes had
dinner with TR. The latter had heard some details about the Dawes
maneuver from George Perkins, a future Progressive party brain
truster and a quietly emerging McKinley-Dawes confidant (who
had been in the White House meeting with McKinley at the time
Dawes called). This made TR want to know more. However, Dawes
recorded in his journal only Roosevelt's comment that "If he could
have had four years more as Governor of New York, he could have
demolished Platt in New York as we think we have demolished Tan-
ner in Illinois."[28] The Machiavellian mind, however, must wonder:
Did a late-hour reformist counterplot help secure the Roosevelt
nomination?

Alas, the notes in Dawes's journal are maddeningly brief. A year
later, the Chicagoan spent a day at the Oyster Bay home of Roosevelt, now vice president, and they discussed the 1904 presidential
nomination. TR expressed concern that the machine would try to
control the New York delegation against him. Dawes said that he
would back Roosevelt in 1904 and thought Illinois would as well,
but that TR could gain from fighting the New York machine just as
McKinley had profited from beating the Illinois machine in 1896.

Two months later, McKinley was dead and Roosevelt had
become president. The veiled reform potential of a second McKinley administration—never quite definable—was lost. No succeeding vice president, however dedicated, lacking his own mandate
and pledged to a static continuity could do what the twice-elected,
powerful McKinley might have worked with his prestige and
understanding of Capitol Hill power and public opinion. Tariff reciprocity, as noted, withered on the vine. Trade statistics didn't come
alive for Roosevelt as they did for the Ohio ironmaster's son. He

had little chance of imposing reciprocity on Congress—and he didn't try.

The trust issue itself may have been muted by McKinley's death. McKinley's biographers agree that action had been gestating in late 1899 and 1900, albeit no one expected Congress to undertake serious attention in the regular preelection session that began in December 1899 or the lame-duck one in December 1900. Fact-finding by the federal United States Industrial Commission appointed in 1898 was stirring interest, but although McKinley cited its unfinished work in speeches, serious legislative attention to trusts would await the full session of the new Congress convening in December 1901.

The jockeying began in 1900, with TR allowed to make campaign speeches recommending publicity of capitalization and profits, taxation of corporations, and "the unsparing excision of all unhealthy, destructive and anti-social elements."[29] Over a September lunch, the president reminded Senator Hanna, who had been defending the trusts, that McKinley's summer letter accepting renomination termed the trusts "dangerous conspiracies . . . obnoxious to the common law and the public welfare" and requiring legislation. Hanna, unenthusiastic, agreed to modify his speeches.[30] Biographer Leech perceived particular importance in Roosevelt's public stance: "His forthright censure of the trusts did much to counterbalance the deference to business which paralyzed Republican leadership on economic questions, and to attract the enthusiastic support of younger and more progressive elements of the party."[31]

Trusts were certainly on McKinley's mind in 1901 as he collected data, discussed the law with his new attorney general (but old friend) Philander Knox, took note of popular apprehension over the new steel and railroad consolidations, and pondered on what premise and how far to proceed. That summer, as Cortelyou recalled, the president said, "This trust question has got to be taken up in earnest, and soon."[32] In August, under the prodding of Progressive Albert Cummins, Iowa Republicans put a plank in their state platform urging "any modification of the tariff schedules that may be required to prevent their affording a shelter to monopoly."[33]

Charles Olcott, an early-twentieth-century McKinley chronicler assisted by Cortelyou, contends that McKinley planned to give trusts equal billing with tariff reciprocity and that this realization underpinned Roosevelt's own attacks in 1902 and thereafter.[34] Leech, also drawing on Dawes and Cortelyou, concluded that the president's 1901 tour, unlike his other trips to the West, was not intended to affect elections: "The President was going to talk to the country about two subjects which had previously been overshadowed by the postwar issues: the control of trusts and the extension of commercial reciprocity. His choice of these subjects implied that, in the political freedom of his second term, McKinley was going to pit the power of the Executive against the power of the Senate."[35] Had McKinley succeeded with an antitrust campaign tied to tariff reciprocity, he might have waved a bigger stick from 1901 to 1904 than TR did.

As for the evolution of federal tax policy, nothing much happened under TR between 1901 and 1904. McKinley, the experienced former Ways and Means Committee chairman, had helped shape the temporary tax increase enacted in 1898 to finance the war with Spain. One inclusion was a progressive tax on inheritances over ten thousand dollars (save for those passing from husband to wife) that reached a top rate of 15 percent for bequests over one million dollars. Other provisions included a tax of 1 percent on all receipts over two hundred thousand dollars of corporations refining oil or sugar (a two-pronged jab at the sugar trust and Rockefeller's Standard Oil), special taxes on banks and brokers, and a stamp tax on checks and drafts, stocks and bonds, insurance policies, and commercial and legal documents, albeit a larger part of the new revenue came from doubled excise taxes on tobacco and alcoholic beverages.[36]

In 1899, McKinley had asked Justice John Marshall Harlan whether the U.S. Supreme Court, which rejected as unconstitutional the income tax enacted in 1893, had ever ruled on Abraham Lincoln's wartime income tax.[37] He also told Dawes that he intended to recommend an income tax.[38]

TR himself first endorsed a progressive inheritance levy in 1906 and a progressive income tax in 1909. Would McKinley have moved any faster? Probably—especially if success with tariff reciprocity looked likely to reduce government receipts enough to require a new revenue source. Lost tariff revenues had explained the income tax provision in the Democrats' ill-fated Wilson-Gorman Tariff Act of 1894. McKinley's own interest as governor in fairer distribution of Ohio's tax burden—the nonpartisan tax revision commission he appointed in 1892, reaching beyond corporate and franchise taxes, had recommended a general levy on intangible wealth!—could have been extended through a kindred commission on the federal level. It might have included the likes of economist Edwin Seligman, an advocate of a progressive income tax who had advised Roosevelt's 1899 deliberations in New York.

Labor would have remained a McKinley theme and ally. In 1897, the new president had refused to appoint as postmaster general a Wisconsin party regular, Henry C. Payne, strongly urged on him by Mark Hanna, because of the man's record as a lobbyist and as an anti-labor employer. Biographer Leech quotes McKinley telling Hanna that "I cannot put a man in my cabinet who is known as a lobbyist."[39] According to another historian, a protracted strike against Payne's Street Railway Company, joined by a public boycott, had "muted the pro-labor image of the Republican Party," which was why McKinley took Robert La Follette's objection over Hanna's pleading.

In a similar vein, Treasury Secretary Lyman Gage of Illinois, picked in 1897 partly because of Dawes's recommendation, had bolted the GOP in 1884 and was a persistent foe of the state GOP machine. After the Haymarket Riot of 1886, Gage had favored pardons for the accused participants and become an advocate of "more friendly consultation and less inconsiderate action on the part of labor and capital."[40] Terence V. Powderly, onetime head of the Knights of Labor, was appointed by McKinley as commissioner general of immigration; AFL chief Gompers and railway union leader Frank Sargent were named to the Industrial Commission.[41] The 1900 GOP platform endorsed Gompers's support of an eight-hour day for government workers. Other former labor union officials had federal appointments under McKinley, several as U.S. consuls in Britain and the continent.

In 1903, Roosevelt signed legislation that McKinley had first put forward to establish a new Cabinet Department of Commerce and Labor. Named to head it was the former president's chief secretary, Cortelyou. Over a full second term, McKinley doubtless would have kept in close touch with the AFL's Gompers, who later commented on their relationship: "He would frequently ask me to the White

House to see him, and I would sometimes ask for the privilege. At no time was I disappointed."[42]

Far from being a reactionary overwhelmed by the approach of the twentieth century, McKinley was arguably a politician ahead of his time. The year 1896, however, was not a time in which progressivism could risk the boldness so easy in 1906 or 1909. According to Midwestern historian Richard Jensen, the conservative countercrusade against Bryan was so stigmatizing that the effects "took years . . . to wear off. Many, if not most, of the [future] Progressive crusaders had battled in the trenches against Bryan, including Robert La Follette, George Norris, Theodore Roosevelt, Jonathan Dolliver, William Allen White, Albert J. Beveridge, Louis Brandeis and Woodrow Wilson. Only when the spectres of Altgeldism and free silver vanished did they feel free to propose reforms again, or to indulge in crusades."[43]

We might add the muckraker Lincoln Steffens, who voted for McKinley, or the socialist author Jack London, who said he would have voted for McKinley if that had been necessary to stop Bryan. Arguably, it was only after Bryan's second defeat in 1900 that the middle class in general and the future leaders of Progressivism would be ready to edge toward controversial reforms—suppression of corporate political contributions, implementation of income and inheritance taxes, direct election of U.S. senators—from the Nebraskan's 1896 crusade. Under TR, the 1901–04 years became a transition period; how much more or less transformation might have come under McKinley can only be guessed.

In the real world, the realignment president whose ethnic and metropolitan inroads greatly enlarged his party's constituency for Progressivism did not live to see that trend catch fire. The Senate never faced his planned challenge. The new Fifty-seventh Congress, to which McKinley would have outlined his not-quite-finished requests, did not arrive in Washington for a regular session until December, six weeks after the president's funeral train had left for Canton.

THE MCKINLEY-ROOSEVELT CONTINUUM

The Ohio-born historian James Ford Rhodes, who happened to be Mark Hanna's brother-in-law, published a volume in 1922 called

The McKinley and Roosevelt Administrations, 1897–1909. He saw parts of the McKinley-Roosevelt continuum, but we can identify many more.

The willingness to remain in office by McKinley's cabinet, which Roosevelt quickly requested, bespoke a rare tribute to the dead president by an especially capable group of men. McKinley had made a few unwise appointments in 1897, especially Russell Alger at the War Department and John Sherman at State. (Woodrow Wilson, too, would make a Sherman-like mistake in 1913 by naming his own party's longtime unsuccessful presidential contender William Jennings Bryan as secretary of state or "premier.") However, the cabinet of 1901—John Hay at State, Elihu Root at War, Lyman Gage at Treasury, Philander Knox as attorney general, "Tama Jim" Wilson at Agriculture, Charles E. Smith as postmaster general, John Long at Navy, and Ethan Allen Hitchcock at Interior—was among the best of the Gilded Age. Their lengthy tenures—Hay, Wilson, and Hitchcock stayed through the entire term, Root and Knox until 1904—helped to ensure that most Rooseveltian policies would develop out of McKinley's. Long and Gage, departing in 1902, were in their late sixties when they left.

Previous vice presidents who became president—Tyler in 1841, Fillmore in 1850, Johnson in 1865, and Arthur in 1881—sought or received no comparable pledges.[44] Majorities of the held-over cabinet members exited soon or were replaced. McKinley's memory and Roosevelt's leadership qualities constituted a unique political adhesive. This is a central part of my emphasis on a McKinley-Roosevelt continuum.

The major shift under Roosevelt come in conservation and care of natural resources. In forestry and reclamation, both TR preoccupations, his interest and attention greatly exceeded those of McKinley, who was neither sportsman nor outdoorsman. Countless forests and national parks bear witness. Yet the latter's secretary of the interior, Ethan Allen Hitchcock, was not only kept on, but served through March 1907. His description in *Who Was Who in American Politics* emphasizes his McKinley antecedents:

Missouri Republican and close friend of President McKinley, who appointed him secretary of the interior (1898–1907), a post in which he quickly and effectively established himself as a conservationist and friend of the Indians. He exposed wide frauds in the handling of public lands, cleaned out the General Land Office, and had more than a thousand people in twenty states indicted, among them many government officials.[45]

As for the trusts, besides the evidence of McKinley's larger preparations, the die may have already been cast under his regime for Roosevelt's most famous move, the *Northern Securities* antitrust case brought by Attorney General Knox in 1902. Having known Knox since the latter's Ohio college days three decades earlier, the president doubtless consulted him on the trust issue, especially because the railroads combining under the Northern Securities banner roiled the stock market in the late spring of 1901, just as Knox was taking up his new post. Their personal and political closeness deserves greater attention.[46] Mark Hanna had told James J. Hill, whose railroads were involved, of the administration's earlier concern. After Knox brought suit in February 1902, Hanna said, "I warned Hill that McKinley might have to act against his damn company last year. Mr. Roosevelt's done it."[47]

Roosevelt's rhetorical calls to arms between 1901 and 1904 were a clarion he was far better equipped to sound than McKinley—the Ohioan's disingenuous techniques forged back in the 1870s were becoming dated. The time had come to mobilize popular and congressional reformation of corporate abuses through open leadership, not quiet backstage orchestration. TR brought an aristocratic outspokenness and aplomb much better suited to this challenge than McKinley's congeniality and middle-class demeanor.

On railroad issues, TR made no splash until his second term, when he led in enacting the Hepburn Act (1906), which gave government the power to set railroad rates. The Elkins Act, passed in 1903, had prohibited rebates to favored shippers. McKinley, who had introduced Granger resolutions as a congressman and pushed railroad regulation as governor of Ohio, would have achieved comparable legislation as the progressive tide rose.

When TR threatened to put coal mines into federal receivership in 1902 after mine-owner recalcitrance in a strike, Hanna was already saying how it would "serve the mine owners right" if the government seized the mines. Private property rights were not sacred to nationalists like McKinley and Hanna. In 1900, as anger grew over the outrageous prices charged by the steel industry for warships' armor plate, the McKinley Navy Department led by Secretary Long had threatened to build its own armor plate facility.[48]

As for TR's growing attention to labor-management relations and arbitration, we must recall that McKinley, two decades earlier, brought about a national arbitration system on the floor of Congress, later enacted a state-level system in Ohio, and quietly, so as not to introduce politics, presided over dozens of arbitrations as governor. Under his prodding, Congress passed the Erdman Act of 1898, which set up wage mediation for interstate railroads. Hanna was cut from surprisingly similar cloth. He boasted, justifiably, that "I was the first employer that I know of in the state of Ohio that ever recognized and treated with organized labor."[49] Rare is the chapter about Hanna that skips his famous rebuke to a Philadelphia banker who called laborers the "lower classes." "Do you mean working men?" said Hanna. "Or do you mean criminals and that kind of people. Those are the lower classes."[50]

In 1901, Hanna became associated with the conciliation and arbitration work of the National Civic Federation, of which Treasury Secretary Gage was honorary president and Samuel Gompers vice chairman. He spent the last two years of his life devoting as much time to coal, steel, and railway labor relations as he did to Senate business. On this issue, Roosevelt and the Square Deal fell in behind the McKinley-Hanna tradition. TR also met with AFL chief Gompers in the White House, but it was McKinley who had opened the door.

The former Rough Rider's cultivation of experts and academic advisers was a fact. However, his willingness to use government-appointed commissions to gather data and point legislators in well-planned directions already had been developed into a political art form by his predecessor, as chapter 6 will examine.

McKinley was also far ahead of TR in supporting the franchise for women, black voting in the South, and direct election of U.S. senators (which he backed in the House of Representatives). Several biographers have made much of TR's controversial invitation to black educator Booker T. Washington to have dinner in the White House. In 1898, McKinley had visited the famous college president in Tuskegee, Alabama, and taken along much of his cabinet. Roosevelt pushed the Vatican to get a cardinal's hat for Archbishop John Ireland of St. Paul, the leading Republican among Catholic prelates. McKinley had built that relationship during a decade when it was much more controversial. And so on.

Nor was TR the real architect of McKinley-era wartime successes and military reforms nor of the decision for the Panama Canal nor the rise of U.S.-British entente. Biographer Gould has rebutted the "fateful telegram" theory that Roosevelt, in a single late February day as acting secretary of the navy, was decisive in readying the U.S. Pacific Squadron for its great victory three months later in Manila Bay:

> The actual sequence of events is more complex, and Roosevelt's message shrinks in importance. Naval planning for an attack on the Philippines dated back to 1895, when the possibility of a Spanish-American conflict over Cuba first arose. . . . In late October 1897 Commodore Dewey was named commander-in-chief of the Asiatic Squadron, and the Philippine plan, whose general outlines he already knew, was available to him in early 1898, when he took over his new assignment. As the Cuban crisis worsened, the navy relayed orders to Dewey in accordance with the plan. On January 27, he was told to retain men whose enlistments had expired. Roosevelt's wire of February 25 was part of this preparatory process.[51]

In a related vein, TR's gush over war as a national fulfillment was such in 1898 that he could add little to the limited imagination of U.S. diplomacy. A more mature Roosevelt might have been able to, one naval historian has noted, "but no one in his right mind would have trusted TR to conduct sensitive diplomacy in 1898."[52] TR's arbitration of the Russo-Japanese War in 1904, for which he received the Nobel Peace Prize, represented a greater maturity and an exposure to McKinley's emphasis—chapter 6 will say more—on elevating arbitration internationally.

Sweeping reform that put the army under a new General Staff, announced by Secretary of War Root in 1903, dated back to the Spanish-American War aftermath. McKinley had cannily picked Root in 1899 for his legal and administrative skills, and the president's de facto wartime chief of staff, Adjutant General Corbin, served as the secretary's military collaborator. Still, according to one military historian, McKinley "gave Root his most vital support . . . and used his influence with Congress to push the reform legislation. While the whole program of army reform was not completed until two years after McKinley's death, his approval and support were essential conditions of its birth."[53]

Roosevelt's brusqueness helped complete British agreement to a new treaty permitting the Panama Canal and its fortification by the United States. However, the substitution of Panama for a Nicaraguan route harked back to 1899 discussions. McKinley had been impressed enough by the case for Panama to arrange a year's delay while Mark Hanna pulled together more information. Hanna read up, accepted the Panamanian argument, and led the spring 1902 congressional debate that shifted the canal's location.

TR, however, was less than skilled in arranging for the right of way. One historian at the U.S. Naval Academy, writing of the Roosevelt-seeded Panamanian revolution, observed, "The 'rape' of Panama from Colombia by Theodore Roosevelt followed McKinley's death and lost the United States the friendship McKinley hoped to cement in that area through another Pan-American Conference."[54]

Although Roosevelt favored Anglo-America entente, his early diplomacy in 1901 and 1902 verged on bluster—bugle calls over U.S.-British canal negotiations and troop dispositions in the Alaska-Canada border dispute. He may have been too unused to carrying a big stick to speak softly at the same time. In *Great Britain and the United States*, his chronicle of the two nations' ties, Oxford historian H. C. Allen concluded, "It was perhaps a good thing for Anglo-American relations that he only came to power when he did, for by 1902, when he had assumed full control, the work of Hay had already been done. . . ." Things had moved along to calm waters, "where presidential ebullience would not have deeply serious consequences."[55]

Even the growth of TR's beloved navy, which he accelerated, began under McKinley. Following up wartime needs, the McKinley naval expansion program of 1900 authorized two battleships, three cruisers, three protected cruisers, and five newfangled submarines.[56] In 1901, McKinley planned to use launching ceremonies for the battleship *Ohio* in San Francisco to speak on the importance of a two-ocean navy, but his activities in San Francisco turned out to be constrained by his wife's sudden illness.[57]

During the four years after the election of 1904, Roosevelt came into his own with a boldness and verve McKinley would have found difficult. The size of TR's landslide, in turn, was a triumph of Progressive enablement. McKinley had blocked the Democrats from reaching political success along a Populist route in 1896 and 1900. In 1904, Roosevelt's success under a Progressive banner, defeating business and financial Democrat Alton Parker by the biggest Republican presidential majority on record, proved the conservative Democratic route even rockier than Bryan's path. Parker carried only one state—Kentucky—outside the old Confederacy, losing the Bryan silver heartland of Colorado, Idaho, Montana, Nevada, and Utah by almost two to one. Even populism was beginning to morph into Republican Progressivism.

Overall, the McKinley-Roosevelt continuum was itself more progressive than conservative, guiding American politics for roughly another decade, finally cresting in the 75 percent of the national presidential vote cast in 1912 for Progressive Democrat Woodrow Wilson, TR as a third-party Progressive, and Socialist Eugene Debs. The hapless Republican, William Howard Taft, received only 23 percent. Not only is this Republican presidential sequence from 1896 to 1912 among the nation's most important, it is one of the least fathomed. In the persons of both McKinley and TR, two different enablers of Progressive politics saddled and rode the nation's conservative party.

Part III

President McKinley in
Retrospect

6

McKinley Reconsidered

> More than any other single individual, William McKinley stood pre-
> eminent during these years [the 1890s]. The record of his achieve-
> ments and fortunes reveals the changes that came to the nation. . . .
> He stood at the top of American politics as the result of his own
> masterful skill and because he was as much the dominant political
> personality of his time as Franklin Roosevelt would become in the
> 1930s.   Lewis Gould, *The Presidency of William McKinley*

By late 1900 and 1901, McKinley bestrode American politics.
Newspapers earlier given to mocking cartoons turned to editorial
worries about the power he had built up in the presidency during
the war with Spain and its aftermath. In 1901, his popularity was
great enough to oblige him to squelch late-spring talk about
according him a third term in 1904.

The goals he would set out for his second term once the new
Congress convened in December 1901—and the serious politicking
he would begin in support—were discussion topics on Capitol Hill.
McKinley, legislators knew, was not a man to jump on a bandwagon
prematurely. Wariness was greatest in the Senate, which had
thwarted or delayed him on first-term objectives from Hawaiian
annexation and international arbitration to tariff moderation and
reciprocity. In contrast to the popularly elected president and House
members, senators were chosen by state legislatures and with this
makeup, the upper chamber had become a burial ground for progressive legislation.

Several of the president's advisers—Secretary of State Hay, special tariff Commissioner Kasson—loathed the Senate Old Guard.
Dawes was not far behind, although for a while he sought an Illinois

seat to aid the administration. McKinley had his own unfond memories—Senators Platt and Quay led the cabal that had opposed his
nomination in 1896. Moreover, besides Sherman, who at retirement
age was a special case, he had been unable to entice another senator,
among a number approached, to join his ticket as vice president in
1896 or 1900 or to take a major cabinet position. Pride, institutional
rivalry, and policy differences all counted. Two of the post-1865
presidents snubbed by the Senate, Hayes and Garfield, had, like
McKinley, been former House members from Ohio. During his
House years, the congressman from Canton had voted for a constitutional amendment to require direct election of U.S. senators.

Biographers have come to regard his last speech to the Pan-
American Exposition in September 1901 as the opening trumpet in
a campaign to enlist Congress, especially the recalcitrant Senate, to
implement tariff reciprocity and confront the trusts. Reciprocity
would come first. The trusts would be faced in 1902, when the
United States Industrial Commission appointed by McKinley in
1898 reported back.

Its recommendations were bold enough—to require federal
incorporation of the largest combinations, refocus antitrust laws on
anticompetitive practices, begin progressive taxation of corporations, establish a permanent federal trade commission to investigate
and disclose corporate practices, and provide federal mechanisms
for voluntary mediation and collective bargaining. Other specific
suggestions were to ban child labor, establish an eight-hour day for
federal employees, and reform the courts' use of labor injunctions.
The experts, businessmen and labor allies largely selected by
McKinley—not by Theodore Roosevelt, not by Woodrow Wilson—
wound up laying out much of what would be the Progressive corporate and antitrust agenda through 1914. Similarly, McKinley's
tariff objectives previewed the Payne-Aldrich (1909) and Underwood (1913) Tariffs and were much bolder with respect to reciprocity.

Would the Senate have accepted plans strongly propounded by
McKinley over the three-and-a-half-year period leading up to the
1904 presidential election? Probably enough, at least, to over-
shadow what Roosevelt achieved in those same years. Would TR
himself have won two consecutive terms in 1904 and 1908 and

completed the job? Probably. Would history's relative rankings of William McKinley and Theodore Roosevelt be quite different? Very likely.

However, it was not to be. Instead, the chronicler of McKinley's truncated presidency is obliged to deal with questions left unresolved by his assassination—his leadership qualities, the nature of the masks that he wore—before venturing a larger retrospect.

THE MASKS OF LATE-NINETEENTH-CENTURY U.S. POLITICAL LEADERSHIP

McKinley's lackluster ratings halfway down the list of U.S. presidents have been fed and sustained by stereotypes—the small-town Ohio Mason and Methodist who read the Bible to his invalid wife (and read practically nothing else), the straddler and trimmer ever chasing public opinion, the compliant chief executive unwilling to tangle with the big-business concerns he served. Still, several such images have persisted because they had at least a facade of truth or, more persuasively, roots in the president's own tactics.

Biographers offer several explanations, beginning with the widespread tendency among earlier chroniclers to misread a basic McKinley personality trait—his seeming agreeability and compliant nature. Others have misinterpreted the traits of patience, sympathy, and reassurance he developed over twenty-five years in dealing with his epileptic and depression-prone wife. At least as relevant, in a different way, is the argument that McKinley himself wore several masks.

Professor Morgan, in praising McKinley's diplomacy with Spain, regretted that "the standard textbook stereotype still shows him a well-intentioned bungler with no real policy who wished to avoid war but surrendered to public opinion. This view reflects more a lack of information than conscious distortion among scholars. McKinley's personality, his love of indirection, his refusal to conduct public diplomacy, and the shadowy nature of the forces surrounding his policy have made him seem the led rather than the leader."[1]

Seeming uncertainty was one of his favorite consensus-building tools. Elihu Root, his second secretary of war, observed, "I have talked with him [McKinley] again and again before a Cabinet meeting and found that his ideas were fixed and his mind firmly made up. He would then present the subject to the Cabinet in such a way as not to express his own decision, but yet bring about an agreement exactly along the lines of his own original ideas while the members often thought the ideas were theirs."[2] La Follette drew the same conclusion from their years in Congress: "Back of his courteous and affable manner was a firmness that never yielded conviction, and while scarcely seeming to force issues, he usually achieved exactly what he sought."[3]

Another historian praised his talent—"Few men possessed his skill in disarming opponents and in eventually getting his own way"—but noted that by "trimming sail, he appeared to be slow, unsure, hesitant and undecided if not weak."[4] New York's Tom Platt, who called McKinley "much too amiable and much too impressionable to be safely intrusted with great executive office," was stating a widely held misperception.[5]

In biographer Morgan's view, "the tragedies of his personal life and the necessities of his profession veneered his whole life with a layer of charm and personal kindness so sincere that he thought of others first even as he lay dying."[6] Lewis Gould, however, added that "because he had so many friends, McKinley faced the charge that he had no firm convictions and that he gained affection and popularity by being weak and compliant."[7] In politics—and in Washington especially—kindness is easily mistaken for weakness.

His self-effacement, even more rare in a president, was also misunderstood as weakness. "Elihu Root, John Hay, Theodore Roosevelt, and scores of other people who worked with McKinley remarked on this aspect of his character," according to Morgan.[8] The president didn't care if he got the credit or someone else did, as long as the job got done: "he never enhanced his power at the price of other men's reputations; nor did he take credit where it was not his due."[9]

High drama, though, was uncommon. "The President's adversaries lost," observed Gould, "but after innumerable minor wounds rather than one decisive stroke. While the process of attrition continued, patience seemed to be evasion, maneuvering to be irresolution, and compromise to be defeat. Sometimes these harsh judgments were true; usually they were not."[10] While making fewer enemies, this technique also won fewer laurels.

Often choosing to keep his specific policy views and intentions blurry, McKinley set very little down on paper. These several images—tactics that resembled pliability and lack of conviction, kindly Midwestern affability, lack of drama, distaste for direct confrontation, and a dearth of public and private papers to embroider policy goals and intentions—congealed after his premature death to allow the portraiture of a much lesser man than the achievements during his tenure suggested.

The demands of his wife's illness and the two to three hours he spent with her most days seem to have changed his behavior, making him something of a stoic and driving him more deeply into a private self. Her insistence on attending Washington social functions added to the stress as he would sometimes have to deal with seizures by carrying her from the room and then resuming his place as if nothing had happened.

Already taciturn, McKinley developed iron self-control, which helps to explain how much he managed to achieve in the long hours he worked—caring for his wife, attending cabinet meetings, seeing many visitors, preparing most of his own speeches and messages to Congress, making the key decisions in the State Department during the worsening senility of Secretary Sherman, and all but running the War Department during the difficult months of 1898 and 1899. No amiable mediocrity could have done it; public admiration was not misplaced.

His rectitude was acknowledged even by his opponents. "Their only recourse," said one chronicler, "was to paint his virtues as too perfect, a source of weakness and vacillation. Unable to deny him uprightness, they denied him power. In this rendering, at its most savage in Homer Davenport's cartoons for the New York *Journal*, McKinley became an overdressed Buddha, the smiling, impotent, unidimensional 'virtuous man' manipulated by the strings of others. This image drew far less response from McKinley's contemporaries than from later historians of the period."[11]

Biographers agree that those genuinely close to McKinley admired him and his abilities. Joseph Barstow, an assistant postmaster general who later became a U.S. senator from Kansas, wrote, "No man has ever been president who got such firm hold on the affections of those with whom he came into close personal relations."[12] The few exceptions are easily explained.[13]

Theodore Roosevelt called McKinley "a statesman singularly gifted to unite the discordant forces of government and mold the diverse purposes of men toward progressive and salutary action."[14] To Charles Dawes, working for McKinley was the greatest privilege of his career. Elihu Root and Robert La Follette, as we have seen, praised McKinley and dismissed the idea that he was any kind of follower. John Hay, who collected Renaissance paintings, said in 1896, "I was more struck than ever with his mask. It was a genuine ecclesiastical face of the fifteenth century. And there are idiots who think that Mark Hanna will run him."

Which brings us back to the issue of "the masks that he wore," although different references have employed the term differently. In his early days in Congress, McKinley was thought to look like Napoleon. Hay evoked a Borgia or Medici cardinal. William Allen White called his demeanor "carefully calculated" but could not find "the real man back of that plaster cast that was his public mask."[15] One historian, Richard H. Bradford, has written an unpublished paper: "Mask in the Pageant: William McKinley and American Historians."

Masks there clearly were. Drawing out cabinet officers with ersatz uncertainty was one. His inscrutability on personal matters, especially his wife's condition, was another. Julia Foraker, wife of the Ohio senator, counted the mask of husbandly dedication, although genuine, as particularly effective in political terms. The American public, she wrote, wove "a halo for . . . [McKinley] out of his devotion to his invalid wife. . . . Whatever the qualities, the circumstances, that led him to the highest pinnacle of fame, the thing that endeared McKinley to the nation was his slavish protectiveness toward the woman to whom the best had been given—and taken away."[16]

McKinley's attention to Congress and his desire to look amiable and unthreatening were another mask, although the conservative stalwarts in the Senate saw through parts of it. In 1897, when the Senate had balked at both Hawaiian annexation and an international arbitration treaty with Britain, the president had simply moved on. A year later, after the war with Spain, he prevailed over

Hawaii and in getting a peace treaty ratified, but the Senate continued to block his trade reciprocity agreements. However, had McKinley pushed too boldly too quickly, the Senate would have dealt with him as it had with Hayes, Garfield, Harrison, and Cleveland. During his first term, in Morgan's words, "The need to persuade not command, to walk not stride, denied him the eloquence so common to reformist politicians, and he seemed more passive."[17] Not until 1901, with his reelection mandate in his pocket, did he seem to move toward a stride-and-command posture.

The Senate's late-nineteenth-century supremacy over presidents was an institutional challenge. Others involved ideology. The future president's basic thinking went back to the formative period of the Civil War and its aftermath. In the 1860s and 1870s, many of his positions mirrored the GOP's so-called Radical wing. Many of its leaders were self-made men of evangelical religion—not least Methodists—and hailed from fast-growing areas like Pennsylvania and the Middle West. They have been described as strong "small *d*" democrats who believed in universal suffrage, the rule of the majority, firm reconstruction of the South, high tariffs to support high wages for labor, and greenbacks or other "soft" money approaches to avoid economic contraction.[18] McKinley fit the pattern.

Several years after reaching Congress, he became a protégé of a man who had symbolized Radical thinking: William D. "Pig Iron" Kelley of Pennsylvania, who served as chairman of the House Ways and Means Committee under GOP majorities in the 1880s. In the late sixties and seventies, Kelley had championed Negro suffrage, harsh Reconstruction, greenbacks, a shorter workweek, and tariff protection. In 1872, he had helped to push through the House a bill, later blocked in the Senate, to create a federal commission to study the wages and hours of labor and the division of profits between labor and capital.[19] In 1878, Kelley was one of very few Republicans in the House to be elected with a simultaneous Greenback endorsement.

The year 1872 probably marked the peak of GOP attention to labor. That year, the Republicans even staged a sham "National Workingmen's Convention" in New York to renominate President Grant along with his new running mate, pro-labor Massachusetts Senator Henry Wilson, the onetime "Natick Cobbler." Beginning in

1873, as the United States slid into an economic depression that was painful through 1878, the mood of the American opinion-molding classes began to shift.

Harsh times brought conflict that eroded middle-class support for workers and unions. Corporations demanded government help. Troops began to be used to break up strikes, most conspicuously in 1877. This same period saw swelling American enthusiasm for the theories of Herbert Spencer, whose so-called social Darwinism proclaimed a survival of the fittest and rejected attempts to ease the lot of the unsuccessful. Laissez-faire economics enjoyed a more or less overlapping heyday. By 1896, both credos were weakening, but the vituperation of the upper and professional classes against Bryan and the "mob" created a new disdain for reform. Such were the two decades in which McKinley served as a member of Congress, governor of Ohio, and then president. Politics in Lincoln's democratic and pro-labor mode had not regained fashion, even if streaks of it remained appealing in the Middle West.

Some early GOP Lincoln supporters, as well as Republican Radicals of the late 1860s—separate groups, despite some overlap—soured enough to leave the party during the 1870s and 1880s: David Davis of Illinois, Wendell Phillips of Massachusetts, and James Weaver of Iowa, for example. However, most officeholders stayed on, shading older views. Kelley was one, and on some counts, as we have seen, so was Rutherford Hayes—the two men that McKinley, as an imminent presidential contender, eulogized with the greatest respect and affection when they died between 1890 and 1893.

The resemblance of these disgruntlements to McKinley's own thinking was beyond coincidence. The pro-labor and tax redistribution policies he quietly brought to fruition as governor in early 1890s Ohio were tougher than those that roused the Platt organization to remove Theodore Roosevelt as governor of New York in 1900. Economists later known as Progressives wrote pamphlets for McKinley (John Bates Clark) or during his presidency held senior posts in the Interstate Commerce Commission and Bureau of Labor Statistics. Not only did McKinley appoint labor leaders to federal posts but, according to Dawes, he allowed the railway unions a veto over at least one of his ICC nominations.[20]

Wall Street had wanted someone other than McKinley in 1896; and in 1898, when one congressman in a visiting delegation charged him "with doing Wall Street's bidding" in avoiding war, he replied, "[M]y whole life is an answer to that statement."[21] By 1901, Old Guard tariff stalwarts had begun to wonder if the author of the McKinley Tariff might turn out to be the most effective critic of strict protection.

On such matters, McKinley set little down on paper and sought no coverage in the newspapers. He was an enormously popular Republican, a successful war president, a man of seemingly amiable, unthreatening demeanor, and a middle-class Mason and Methodist who most nights read the Bible to his wife. That may have been the ultimate mask of the old egalitarian Radical as reform gathered itself for the new century.

MCKINLEY AND INSTITUTIONAL INNOVATION

Unlike most conservative presidents of the late nineteenth century, McKinley quickly set about using his office to rebuild the power lost by the executive branch since Lincoln. As commander in chief, the former army private who had capitalized the spelling of *government* back in 1861 sought to resurrect the force that he had admired. The machine leaders he beat for the nomination had their Washington headquarters in the U.S. Senate, as did more than a dozen millionaire industrialists able to control or buy their state legislatures. The Senate, by most accounts, was the body to which the power lost by the executive over two decades had migrated.

In 1896, with this in mind, McKinley had hoped to enlist Iowa Senator William Allison as his running mate. Besides his credibility with the Republican party's silver bloc, Allison was an influential Senate GOP insider. As vice president, presiding over the Senate, he could have helped the new administration. Even Vice President Hobart, a New Jersey politician new to Washington, wound up as the president's eyes and ears in the Senate over which he presided. After Hobart's funeral, McKinley remarked to Dawes, "Hobart attained an influence which made him one of the great factors" in the struggle for administration policy. Hobart also deputized for the president in cabinet relations—as in carrying the word to Secretary of War Russell Alger when it was time for the latter to resign. As one biographer noted, "[T]he partnership between the two men had revitalized the office of vice president."[22]

One of the carrots dangled before Theodore Roosevelt in 1900 was this growing role for the vice president. This was confirmed quickly enough when McKinley stayed home and TR got to be the national ticket's lead campaigner, basking in the huge crowds. Increased importance for the vice president obviously helped to rebuild the overall executive branch.

McKinley had other tactics for dealing with the Senate. When that body seemed unlikely to pass a treaty to annex Hawaii in 1898, he harked back to the precedent of Texas in 1846, taken into the United States by a joint resolution of Congress (which did not require the two-thirds majority needed for a treaty). When the president was rounding up support for a tight Senate vote on the treaty ending the war with Spain and giving new territory to the United States, aides got several state legislatures to pass pro-treaty resolutions to influence their senators' votes in Washington.

But most frequently, McKinley gained advantage by establishing commissions to assemble the critical decision-making information on vital issues that Congress or just the treaty-making Senate would face. Senators as well as outside experts were often picked as members, with an eye to enlisting them to sell the commission's eventual recommendations to their colleagues. McKinley did this with considerable success on bimetallism, Hawaii, peace with Spain, the Philippines, and relations with Canada (a joint high commission). Three border-state and Southern Democrats—Gray of Delaware, Faulkner of West Virginia, and Morgan of Alabama— were wooed into the White House orbit, in chronicler Leech's words, by McKinley "flagrantly using them as Executive agents and committing them to support Executive action."[23]

Indignation over tampering with the separation of powers was such that in 1899, New Hampshire Republican Senator William E. Chandler introduced a resolution forbidding the practice. McKinley talked him into dropping the resolution and resumed naming commissions, albeit with more attention to Senate resentment.

Other presidents before McKinley had appointed commissions, but he gave the device much greater usage. In Ohio, where the governor could only suggest, not veto, he had taken control of the debate over unfair distribution of tax burdens in 1892 by appointing an expert commission to recommend solutions, as Roosevelt would later do in New York. The United States Industrial Commission, launched in 1898, performed a similar federal-level task with respect to trusts—in a sense usurping legislative prerogatives by assembling expert opinions and catalyzing proposals that Congress would not have initiated. McKinley, more than TR, was the innovator in assembling policy-making experts—for example, appointing Professor Dean Worcester of Michigan University to his first Philippine Commission because of his research in the islands and then naming Professor Bernard Moses of California to his second Philippine Commission after reading his books on Spanish government.

His use of patronage was also clever. Some have criticized his civil service policies for appearing to retreat from Cleveland-era reforms, but McKinley restored to political appointment some of the senior federal departmental staff positions needed for executive branch effectiveness and Washington clout. Cleveland, of course, was less interested in asserting executive power or activist government.

Autumn congressional and gubernatorial electioneering was another McKinley innovation. The last president to tour, Andrew Johnson in 1866, had come a cropper, but McKinley, after remaining in the White House in 1897, ventured out boldly in 1898 and 1899. The first year had the congressional midterm elections, but 1899 had its smaller share of statehouse, legislature, and (indirectly) Senate seats at stake. The benefits of McKinley's campaigning in 1898 were clear enough by late October that the Republican Congressional Committee revised downward its midmonth projection of party losses.[24] The following year, with the president on the hustings in the Midwest, the Republicans won all of the non-Southern governorships being filled—Iowa, Massachusetts, Ohio, and Rhode Island— and counted enough Buckeye state legislators to return Mark Hanna to the Senate. Legislators recognized the implications of presidential coattails.

House Speaker Thomas Reed, bitter at McKinley's success in the war and in retaining the Philippines, found his leadership in tatters and resigned his speakership and House seat in mid-1899. Representative David Henderson of Iowa, much more amenable to the policies of the president, was chosen as Speaker. The Republicans would wind up holding the House of Representatives from 1895 to 1911, their longest hegemony since the Civil War years.

The presidential "bully pulpit" was as much a McKinley as a Roosevelt example. If autumn campaign tours provided a new presidential forum, McKinley also greatly improved White House press relations and coverage. By making the White House and its war room the hub of 1898 military strategy, he raised its importance as a center of news dissemination. So did the skill of Cortelyou, an embryonic press secretary, in coordinating the flow and release of major presidential speeches and messages.[25] "Under McKinley," concluded biographer Gould, "relations between the press and White House took on a formal character from which a regular role for journalists would evolve."[26] Cultivation of the press began in June, a month after the battle of Manila Bay, when efforts were made by the Vanderbilts to bar reporters from a McKinley visit to one of the family mansions. The word came back: no press, then no presidential visit. Six months later, the first official White House reception for the press was scheduled shortly after Christmas.[27]

Far from being an accident, the rise in McKinley's popularity and power reflected political shrewdness of a kind long missing in the White House.

ARBITRATION, MEDIATION, AND UNIFICATION

Even in the army and in Congress, McKinley had been more mediator than gladiator. Several of his biographers emphasize his commitment, dating back to the War for the Union, to strengthening national unity, ecumenicalism, and a politics of inclusiveness. In his eyes, the Republicans were the party that had saved the Union. Blacks should be entitled to vote because so many had fought for the flag. A sense of nationalism akin to that of Alexander Hamilton or Henry Clay underpinned McKinley's belief in the protective tariff system as one that built and strengthened America.[28] Another historian, citing his care for his wife, found McKinley pursuing "as his special task the diminution of dissensions in his private life and the life of the nation."[29]

McKinley's ascent along this half-psychological pathway of his politics is as striking as his climb toward the brass ring of presidential politics and his quarter-century transformation on tariff issues. In his late twenties, as president of the Canton YMCA, he emphasized Christian ecumenicalism; in his thirties, he spoke in Congress for a national system of labor arbitration. As governor of Ohio, not only did he preside over the enactment of the second state labor arbitration system after Massachusetts, but without publicity he helped settle many of the disputes himself.

Despite the well-considered political opportunism of his straddling position on the issue of gold versus silver currency, there is little doubt that as president, he sought to reduce the fissure between West and East. His work for an international agreement on bimetallism had this intention. To woo the West, the accompanying presidential commission of 1897 was chaired by Colorado U.S. Senator Edward Wolcott, a silverite Republican.

In his inaugural, McKinley had spoken of ending the discord between North and South, and by the close of the hostilities with Spain in 1898, he waxed fulsome. "Whatever else this war has done," he told a South Dakota audience in 1899, "there is a result for which we should all offer thanksgiving and praise—it has unified every section. We now, almost for the first time in our history, know no North, no South, no East, no West, but are all for a common country."[30] At least he wished it so.

Ironically, one of his challenges as president in 1897 involved international comity: a treaty for the arbitration of differences between the United States and Britain. The treaty was negotiated by the Cleveland administration, and McKinley endorsed it after taking office, given his long interest in arbitration. The Senate rejected it by three votes under the needed two-thirds support, but henceforth his interest in arbitration would extend to the international level.

In 1899, after the czar of Russia had proposed a conference on disarmament and international arbitration, McKinley sent a U.S. delegation to The Hague for negotiations that led to what became the Permanent Court of Arbitration. In his annual message to Congress, the president urged the Senate to ratify the treaty establishing the court, which it proceeded to do.

Before the war with Spain in 1898, McKinley had offered himself—unsuccessfully—as a mediator between Madrid and the Cuban rebels. In 1900, to no avail, he offered to mediate between Britain and the Boer insurgents in South Africa.

The Western Hemisphere, however, provided a more fertile field. As a congressman in the 1880s, he had been an avid supporter of Pan-Americanism, and was one of those responsible for calling the First Inter-American Conference of American States in 1889.[31] With McKinley in the White House, Chile and Argentina in 1899, after averting war over a frontier dispute, accepted U.S. arbitration, which successfully settled the matter. In his message to Congress that December, the president suggested that a second inter-American conference be held, which was agreed to and set for 1901 in Mexico City. Held shortly after McKinley's assassination, its participants deemed *mandatory* arbitration excessive, and the American states became parties to The Hague Convention of 1899 and the Permanent Court of Arbitration, which provided a voluntary resort.

Trade reciprocity should be thought of as a corollary to McKinley's Pan-Americanism. Many of the treaties and agreements negotiated between 1898 and 1900 were within the hemisphere—with Nicaragua, Ecuador, and the Dominican Republic, as well as with Great Britain for her West Indian colonies and Denmark for Saint Croix. The Pan-American Exposition in 1901, where the president was assassinated, had been his venue of choice for setting out a principal second-term objective: "The period of exclusiveness is past. The expansion of our trade and commerce is the pressing problem. Commercial wars are unprofitable. A policy of good will and friendly trade relations will prevent reprisals. Reciprocity treaties are in harmony with the spirit of the times; measures of retaliation are not."

As governor of Ohio, McKinley had maintained inclusiveness by gender and race. Women won the right to vote in school board elections in 1894. Black leaders applauded his help; and in an era when lynchings were rising almost unchecked, McKinley sent troops to Washington Court House, in southern Ohio, to prevent the lynching of a convicted black prisoner. The soldiers were obliged to fire on a crowd and killed two. Still, as president between 1897 and 1901, McKinley's earlier commitment to black equality weakened as his practical attention shifted to the reunification of North and South, East and West.

The commitment McKinley insisted on upholding involved black opportunities in the military. Black soldiering in the Civil War had been a pillar of his support of their political equality afterward, and he insisted on that chance again in 1898. Over War Department objections, he required that black regiments be allowed to fight in the Philippines with black field grade officers. In an 1899 speech in Savannah, Georgia, he mentioned that (ex-Confederate) General Wheeler was on hand and "can tell you better than I can of the heroism of the black regiments that fought [in Cuba] side by side with the white troops on those historic fields." Many Southern whites did not like these words, but it was a commitment McKinley would not retract.

Otherwise, beyond the usual Republican administration's quota of federal jobs for blacks, McKinley did not do much. The contrary national tide was strong. In 1893, a Democratic Congress had passed and Grover Cleveland had signed legislation repealing the federal enforcement laws that still nominally constrained Southern disenfranchisement of blacks. In 1896, the U.S. Supreme Court had upheld segregation in the case of *Plessy* v. *Ferguson,* and in 1898, it upheld new Mississippi election laws in the *Williams* case. "With all that against him," contended biographer Gould, "presidential gestures from McKinley would have produced only the smallest incremental improvements for black people."[32] Probably so; Roosevelt, who doubted black equality, did less, and Woodrow Wilson, who supported segregation, less than TR.

U.S. statesmen sought their moral encomiums further afield. In the years ahead, Theodore Roosevelt turned more of his own attentions overseas, winning the Nobel Peace Prize in 1906 for his mediation of the Russo-Japanese War. Two other close McKinley advisers, Elihu Root and Charles Dawes, would win or share Nobel Peace Prizes in 1912 and 1925. No historian has ever examined how much of this was, at least in part, a legacy of what McKinley began.

THREE MCKINLEY REALIGNMENTS

The political one has already been examined. McKinley's Republican predecessors over two decades had taken office already crippled by their manner of selection, while Democrat Grover Cleveland growled about integrity, cherished an outdated small-government mentality, offended Congress, and picked fights likely to wreck his party. McKinley, by contrast, was the great achiever. He won the Republican nomination unencumbered by obligations, turned his epochal victory over Bryan into a party realignment, and confirmed it four years later. Excluding Kentucky, every state that McKinley carried in 1896 remained Republican until 1912. So did the Senate, and Republicans held the South through the election of 1910. Theodore Roosevelt was not the principal architect; William McKinley was.

The first Roosevelt administration (1901–04) was in many ways the second McKinley administration. Besides keeping McKinley's policies, TR kept McKinley's cabinet. He also favored and promoted talented McKinleyites long after he had to. His choice for vice president in 1904 was Senator Charles Fairbanks of Indiana, in 1896 the leader of McKinley forces in that state, chairman of the 1896 GOP convention, and from 1897 to 1901 a McKinley friend and spokesman in the Senate. Roosevelt's national campaign manager in 1904 was George Cortelyou, McKinley's chief White House secretary. In 1903, TR had made Cortelyou his secretary of commerce and labor; in 1907, he named him secretary of the Treasury. McKinley's close friend, William R. Day, acting secretary of state during the Spanish-American War, received one of TR's three U.S. Supreme Court appointments in 1903. It is tempting to say that TR understood who had built the political house in which he lived.

Realignment presidents have usually furnished or nurtured much of their party's national talent pool over the next generation, and McKinley was no exception. Appendix B on page 163 lists twelve whose service ran as far into the future as 1929 (the expiration of the term of Vice President Charles G. Dawes). The three-sentence profiles give some sense of the caliber of McKinley's principal advisers and the worth of the compliments they paid to him long after his death.

The second McKinley realignment involved the economy, which

in 1897 and 1898 left behind a painful quarter century marked by frequent severe downturns and recurrent debates over gold versus silver and the protective system versus free trade. The result was roughly a decade of prosperity (1897–1907) until the downturn in the latter year. Economically as well as politically, much was consolidated in the United States during this decade.

For all their archaic sound a century later, two props of that new prosperity were the gold standard and the accelerating global industrial lead—crowned by stunning export growth—achieved by the United States under the protective system that McKinley, perhaps more than anyone else, nurtured to this capping success. The gold standard, promoted if not imposed by Britain since the mid-nineteenth century, was a vital mechanism in the economic "globalization" that maximized between 1890 and 1914. The early benefit was to British industrial and export growth, and by 1890, world trade became something of a "gold club," because that was the medium by which most of the bills were paid. McKinley, in his 1890s discussions of the unworkability of free and unlimited coinage of silver at sixteen to one, pointed out that 80 to 90 percent of U.S. trade was with countries on the gold standard or its equivalent.

By the 1890s, of course, joining the Gold Club was essential for a United States—certainly the United States as seen by McKinley and American industry—seeking its prosperity based on production levels too high for domestic consumption alone, which commanded attention to export markets. The cynic who suggests that poor, mediocre McKinley didn't understand such things is absolutely wrong. He talked about them all the time, and in speeches and messages to Congress that he, unlike more recent presidents, wrote himself. John Hay wrote from London in 1897 about the reaction to one of those messages: no European prime minister, he said, could have done as much. The journal of Charles Dawes, who in 1894 had published a textbook on *The Banking System of the United States and its Relation to the Money and Business of the United States*, has page after page of references to the arcane subject matter he discussed with the *president*, not the president's economic advisers.

When McKinley voted for free silver in Congress in 1878, he did so as an Ohio politician—and as an Ohio politician, he was tactically correct. But in the decades to come, he blended political skill with more economic sophistication than is generally realized.

The same can be said of his approach to tariffs and protection. Loyally Ohioan and iron-, steel-, and wool-oriented in 1878, he quickly became much more. Combining shrewdness and a vastly retentive memory with a sweeping, war-forged patriotism, he sought a late-nineteenth-century nationalist version of what Henry Clay had called the "American System" of internal improvements and protected industries seeking a powerful tomorrow. He was sometimes grudging when first introduced to proposed modernizations of the basic protective system, but he invariably came around if he saw a national good. Thus he progressed to supporting a tariff commission for more scientific rate setting (1882), customs reform and bargaining reciprocity (1890), reduced rates (1897, although Congress sidestepped his private urgings), and finally, in 1901, a system that remained only partially protective, to be changed by reciprocity to promote U.S. exports and dismantle high rates helpful to monopolies and anticompetitive behavior.

Timing was everything. McKinley opened himself to change with some boldness, but he pursued it cautiously, like he mounted a political bandwagon. By 1900 and 1901, when he contemplated momentous legislative change, it was because he had already seen a compelling change occur in the circumstances of U.S. trade. Its volume soared after 1897, but especially on the export side. If imports didn't rise to follow, the high-output structure of U.S. industry would be in danger.

If McKinley had boasted a Ph.D., chroniclers might call him a seer. But then he never would have been the practical politician, the man whose power by 1901 could well have accomplished his hopes. His protective-system transformation was the late-nineteenth-century equivalent of the volte-face of the preeminent mid-twentieth-century anti-Communist, Richard Nixon, who pursued the détente with Russia and China in 1972 that no other leader could have orchestrated (or been allowed to). McKinley even chuckled to Cortelyou in 1901 that only the Republicans could seriously revise the tariff because the Democrats had so often mishandled it.[33]

Part of the blindness to McKinley's prowess has involved inattention to the larger role of protective (mercantile or tariff) systems in the evolution of the leading world economic powers of modern times. The last three such—the Dutch Republic, Britain, and the United States—have all used mercantilist or tariff systems or some combination of government promotion and support to rise to that strength and position. Descriptions of early Dutch mercantilism abound, most notably in Jonathan Israel's *Dutch Primacy in World Trade*. British protective practices between the sixteenth century and the 1840s have a thousand chroniclers. Those in the United States have even more.

McKinley's rare, if not unique, competence lay in understanding both the purpose and the validity of the protective phase and the later need to modify it—as the Dutch and British had in their day—to meet changing and globalizing circumstances. Had he survived through 1904, the United States might have had a much more sophisticated system in place than that achieved by the Payne-Aldrich Tariff Act of 1909 or the Underwood Tariff Act reductions of 1913. Moreover, having been orchestrated by so prominent a Republican expert, such changes under McKinley might not have been reversed by subsequent GOP regimes to new and counterproductive heights, as happened through the Fordney-McCumber and Hawley-Smoot Tariff Acts of 1922 and 1930 under Harding and Hoover.

The downside of the era launched by the economic realignment under McKinley was its acceptance of huge trusts and monopolies, along with lopsided and dangerous wealth concentrations. Once the resumption of economic growth seemed secure by 1899 and 1900, however, these were problems he apparently planned to deal with through regulation of the trusts, as well as by whatever income taxation could be managed within the framework of the Supreme Court's crippling 1895 ruling.

With respect to the third realignment under McKinley—the rise of the United States to world power and a de facto alliance with Britain that sent Anglo-America victorious through two world wars—some at the dissenting voices raised points akin to those argued in dismissing the gold standard and tariff realpolitik, despite their benefits at the time. What began in Asia, critics said, was imperialism, a pathway the United States never should have taken, a mistake that in Asia ultimately led to the jungles, dishonor, and disillusionment of Vietnam.

There is that later connection. But there are also many others. To begin with, the notion that the United States should not and need not have followed the expansionist pathway in the 1890s and especially after the war with Spain is unrealistic. Americans are moral, geographic, and commercial rainbow chasers.

Territorially, the history of the English-speaking peoples since the Tudors and of Americans specifically since the first settlement is one of almost relentless expansionism. On top of which, the imperial milieu of the late nineteenth century so captured the Western mind that not just Britain and France sought to stake out every sub-Saharan scrub, Caribbean reef, and Micronesian atoll. Spain, Portugal, and Holland cherished the bits of the overseas past they could still hold, and even Sweden (Saint Bart's), Denmark (Saint Croix and the rest of the Danish West Indies), and Belgium (the Congo) managed a tropical fort or two. Although Russia pulled back from northern California in the early nineteenth century and sold Alaska in 1867, the czar kept busy gobbling up the Caucasus and central Asia. Germany took almost anything available. Even before Mussolini talked of mare nostrum, Italians dreamed of Caesar as their warships anchored off Libya, Ethiopia, and Eritrea.

That Americans would not participate is unrealistic. That they would do so with relative republican sympathies and comparative humanitarianism is reasonably factual. Of the four overseas territories taken, occupied, or annexed in 1898 and 1899, this disposition was made. Hawaii eventually became a state, Puerto Rico a self-governing commonwealth. Cuba, freed from Spain in part for humanitarian reasons, was occupied for several years during which major outlays were made for food, education, and sanitation and then was given its independence. The Philippines was taken, a set of local rebellions put down, and in 1935 it was given self-government and a pledge of independence, which was delayed until 1946 by World War II.

Taking the Philippines in 1898 may not have been the best idea, but as many have written, the choice at the time was more complicated than simply taking or not taking. Had the United States walked away, two interested nations that might have walked in were Germany and Japan. The expansionist position was generally ratified by American voters in the 1898, 1900, 1902, and 1904 elections.

The principal "anti-imperialist" reaction, quite visible in McKinley's own 1896–1900 presidential vote decline, was centered in and around Boston, in some ways resurrecting the earlier mugwump constituency. Wars committing the United States to Mexican, Caribbean, or southeast Asian expansion have usually been least popular in New England.

As an aside, antiexpansionism in general—in particular, the dislike of possessing Hawaii and the Philippines—was prevalent in the South on more rudimentary grounds. Dixie rice and sugar planters worried about cheap Pacific competition. Southern Democrats in Congress stoked existing racial fears. Senator John Daniel of Virginia called the Philippines a racial "witches' cauldron," in which—his citations were somewhat tongue in cheek—travelers were said to have reported spotted and striped people. Champ Clark of Missouri evoked "a Chinese senator from Hawaii, with his pigtail hanging down his back," and Ben Tillman reported that his South Carolina constituents were appalled by the thought of incorporating ten million Filipino "negroes . . . Malays, negritos, Japanese, Chinese, [and] mongrels of Spanish blood."[34] McKinley deplored these statements, but they underpinned a considerable proportion of anti-imperial sentiment.

More broadly, imperialism and anti-imperialism have definite patterns of ebb and flow in Britain and the United States. In the former, once-popular books about imperial Britain's "great game" in India, Afghanistan, and Persia, which went out of fashion after World War II with the collapse of empire, began returning in the 1990s and 2000s as Anglo-American aircraft and missiles subjugated skies from the Persian Gulf to the Khyber Pass. The early U.S. role in the Philippines, unfashionable in the New Deal milieu of the 1930s and again in the 1960s and 1970s because of Vietnam, may also be revisited. A century later, U.S. troops have returned to several southern islands of the archipelago in joint sweeps with local forces against Islamic terrorists.

Other new alignments of the McKinley era had far-reaching importance from the start. His virtual entente with Britain was not popular with Irish-Americans or German-Americans, neither was it much of a national issue. Absent McKinley's formulations, one must wonder, for better or worse, whether even Woodrow Wilson's

Anglophilia (and, for that matter, Theodore Roosevelt's) would have been enough to pull the United States into World War I.

The American fascination with China, renewed in 1900 by the "Open Door" policy, did not pan out commercially in the early twentieth century, but trade between the two countries had exploded by the advent of the twenty-first century. A Japanese-led Asia was seen by many in the 1980s; the wisdom of the twenty-first century is to bet on China and India. To be sure, a latter-day McKinley would be worrying about the jobs being lost in Ohio and elsewhere.

Lastly, the personal attacks on McKinley for his imperialism also founder over his important, but little noted, commitment to international arbitration and mediation. The great imperial powers rarely initiated or accepted such approaches—Britain's refusal of McKinley's proposal to mediate in the Boer War, for example. The moral is that McKinley's instincts for arbitration, pacifism, and humanitarian assistance, well recognized by his biographers, were simply incompatible with full-fledged imperialism. He had too much of a religious and even utopian side. Part of him agreed with Mrs. McKinley's hope that Christian missionaries, even more than Connecticut hardware salesmen, might follow the flag to the Philippines.

A NEAR-GREAT PRESIDENT?

McKinley has to be so regarded, for both his skill and the success of the three realignments or transformations over which he presided. Particularly impressive witness to his capacities, determinations, and strengths of character can be gleaned from the comments, tributes, and recollections of the members of the Republican talent pool assembled by his administration that remained in place for a generation.

These events might appear to match him with Lincoln and Franklin Roosevelt. Indeed, it is easy to find citations that put his leadership and coalition-building abilities in such company. Woodrow Wilson, as we have seen, compared his foreign policy preeminence to Lincoln's. Henry Adams, though in many ways a critic, opined that McKinley "brought to the problem of American government a solution . . . which seemed to be at least practical and American. He undertook to pool interests in a general trust into which every interest should be taken more or less at its own valuation, and whose mass should, under his management, create efficiency. He achieved very remarkable results."[35]

According to Herbert Croly, the Progressive thinker, "McKinley represented, on the whole, a group of ideas and interests as nearly national as could any political leader of his generation."[36] Twentieth-century political historian Richard Jensen noted that "Franklin Roosevelt perfected McKinley's strategy of inclusive pluralism by giving practically every major economic, ethnic, cultural and regional interest group the recognition and legislation it wanted; in the process the Democrats recaptured the support of the liturgical and metropolitan electorate that had formed the key to McKinley's coalition."[37] Did McKinley parallel FDR or, given the chronology, was it vice versa?

To be sure, the Lincoln and FDR analogies are partially rebutted by McKinley's indirect methodologies, middle-class demeanor, and tactical inability to inspire Americans with vision from a pulpit. This is so despite the rare late-nineteenth-century circumstances that justified his indirection and the muted vision. No pulpit was plausible unless and until McKinley was ready to confront the Senate. The great moment of leadership was probably at hand in 1901. But "probably," in this sort of retrospect, is not quite enough.

Once McKinley is left off the list of the handful of great presidents, the question then becomes whether he belongs with the next six to eight, variously described as "very good" or "near great." Here the case is strong, especially because of the achievements and realignments to which he is linked—and which do not depend on where his frequent mask donning and calculated ambiguity is ranked on the spectrum of presidential demeanor. A chief executive does not accomplish what McKinley did, realigning so much among such difficulty, without belonging in this second tier.

Unfortunately, the tendency is for presidents who have been assassinated or have died in office to be lionized—Lincoln, FDR, and John F. Kennedy—or dismissed (Harrison, Taylor, Garfield, McKinley, and Harding). The choice seems to be either Valhalla or potter's field. McKinley has been in the second category, but the great success of his four and a half years in office ought to lift him out, and the fruitful future cut short by his assassination deserves its own examination.

So, in particular, does his relative place among the four presidents—Cleveland, McKinley, TR, and Taft—who managed the nation's 1892–1912 transformation from a continental frontier to a global frontier. Their roles were vital. If we can allocate the credit given to them by twentieth-century historians, it might go as follows: TR 40 percent, Cleveland 30 percent, McKinley 15 percent, Taft 15 percent.

A better calculus would be to rate McKinley and TR evenly at 35 percent and give Cleveland 15 percent and Taft 15 percent. As between McKinley and Roosevelt, the former shaped the Republican realignment and deserves credit for putting in place many of the policy shifts attributed to TR. The latter, however, pulls even because of his *joie de combat* and unique effects through blistering rhetoric, 1904–08 policy making, and a 1912 independent presidential candidacy that divided the GOP and gave Progressivism its political and legislative high-water mark.

Taft, in his way, brought almost as much reformism into the GOP as Roosevelt had and was not the standpatter that TR portrayed. Unfortunately, TR's flamboyance and ability to hog contemporary attention and fascinate latter-day biographers has worked like a pump to suck historical attention away from predecessor and successor alike. But in practical terms, the fact that the three-hundred-pound Taft, as the Republican incumbent, actually trailed the independent TR in the 1912 presidential vote is determinative. The Bull Moose gored the Bewildered Elephant on the hustings— and thereafter in historical memory, too.

Grover Cleveland ranks with Taft as an honest but not momentous president. His most important role lay not with his legislative successes but with his political missteps, even if some had an element of courage. During his first term (1885–89), Cleveland spotlighted the tariff issue, which later broke decisively for the Republicans and McKinley in the nineties. Then during his second term (1893–97), eschewing activist government, he became a symbol of hard times, injudiciously splitting his party down the middle in the gold versus silver currency debate. Not a little of his supposed "courage" was actually ineptitude, and he left the presidency in shreds. Like Taft, he was less important for his achievements than for what his failures set in motion.

The ratings of American presidents have been posted, principally by academicians, in something less than a vacuum of partisan, ideological, or stylistic bias. Great or near-great conservatives seem to gain that recognition from achievements that can only be called unconservative—leading rebel forces in the American Revolution (Washington), voicing the Emancipation Proclamation and leading a civil war to end slavery (Lincoln), or captaining the Progressive uprising against monopolies, trusts, and political corruption (TR). Otherwise, John Adams gets honorable mention as a founding father, but the rest tend to slide.

By this yardstick, McKinley has suffered along with three other Republican presidents who were elected to two terms but were associated with middle-class values and middle-class constituencies: Dwight Eisenhower, Richard Nixon, and Ronald Reagan (although the Watergate scandals put Nixon into a separate category). Clearly, such presidencies do not qualify for greatness. But it seems arguable that the consolidators among them, and much of that stands out in McKinley's desire to heal, renew prosperity, and reunite, deserve a subcategory and criteria of their own. Of these, McKinley, also a realigner, seems most deserving of promotion into near-great ranks.

Of course, there is the hidden McKinley, the egalitarian who ran with the Grangers and promoted women's rights, the "people's candidate" who beat the Eastern bosses, the man who wouldn't have a lobbyist in his cabinet, the cautious reformer who was on the verge of leading a fight to curb the trusts, reform the tariff system, and reenact a progressive income tax. This is the McKinley that brings the hints of Lincoln and FDR to the second-tier credentials of the Republican consolidators. This is the McKinley that might have surprised Americans in that second term he had barely started.

Appendix A:
McKinley in Memoriam

The visitor to Ohio in search of William McKinley's legacy will be surprised by the size of the several memorials to him. Seven men born in the Buckeye State became president of the United States between 1868 and 1920, and the homes of the five living in Ohio when they were elected—Hayes, Garfield, McKinley, Taft, and Harding—have all become historic sites. McKinley, however, is the one who has two major memorials, one in Niles and an especially large and impressive one in Canton. Clearly, McKinley was the Ohio president whom Ohioans expected to be remembered as one of the nation's most important chief executives.

Revealingly, McKinley's major biographers have also described the mourning after his assassination and death in similar terms—the sort of recognition-cum-outpouring given only to important presidents who have made a particular mark. The following draws from the final paragraphs in the biography by Margaret Leech and several appropriate paragraphs—which seem slightly overdrawn—from the final volume of Charles S. Olcott's biography.

MARGARET LEECH, *IN THE DAYS OF MCKINLEY* (1959)

Before the black-column newspapers thudded against the doorways, the people had heard the bells tolling heavily in the night. . . . There were five more days of mourning, of crepe-shrouded buildings and tolling bells and newspapers barred in black, while McKinley's bier traveled from the services to the rites at Washington and then to the resting place at Canton. . . . Never in history had the union of the States been joined in such universal sorrow. North and South, East and West, the people mourned a father and friend, and the fervent strains of "Nearer, My God to Thee" floated like a prayer and a leave taking above the half-masted flags in every city and town. When at last McKinley's casket was carried from the white frame house in Canton, five minutes of silence ruled the land, all traffic and business suspended, while the people bowed in homage to the President who was gone.

CHARLES S. OLCOTT, *THE LIFE OF*
WILLIAM MCKINLEY, Vol. 2 (1916)

Both national and international sympathy found wide expression. Messages of condolence came from every quarter of the globe. Every foreign newspaper of importance printed sympathetic and in most instances appreciative editorials. Memorial sermons were preached in churches of all denominations in every section of the country. Throughout the British Empire there were demonstrations of sincere respect for the memory of the American President. King Edward ordered his court into mourning and commanded that a memorial service be held in Westminster Abbey, where he was personally represented by the highest dignitary of his court. In St. Paul's Cathedral, the service was almost the same as that for Queen Victoria. In the City Temple an immense throng sang the President's favorite hymns. . . . The stock exchanges were closed, flags were displayed at half mast on the public buildings, and people in all walks of life went about the street in the garb of mourning. Even the drivers of cabs and omnibuses tied little bunches of crepe to their whips. The guns of Gibraltar fired a salute, the British Embassy at Constantinople held a memorial service, the banks and exchanges of Bombay closed their doors, and the Dominion of Canada suspended their welcome to the heir apparent, the Duke of Cornwall and York, who with his Duchess had just arrived on a visit, in order that all might join with the Republic in her day of mourning. Never before had the British Government paid such marked homage to any foreigner.

Appendix B:
The Eminent McKinleyites

Most of the presidents who have captained America's major political realignments have also been recognized for identifying and promoting a fair part of their party's talent pool over the next generation. Thus, there are the labels of Jeffersonians, Jacksonians, Lincoln men, and Rooseveltian New Dealers. McKinley did as much but has not gotten appropriate credit. Here are short profiles of twelve men he picked for top jobs, men whose subsequent laurels support the praise of McKinley quoted in these pages.

George B. Cortelyou (1862–1940): chief secretary to President McKinley (1900–1); secretary of commerce and labor (1903–4); postmaster general (1905–7); secretary of the Treasury (1907–9).

Charles G. Dawes (1865–1951): comptroller of the currency (1897–1901); director of the Bureau of the Budget (1921–22); author of post–World War I Dawes Plan; cowinner of Nobel Peace Prize, 1925; vice president of the United States (1925–29).

William R. Day (1849–1923): assistant secretary of state (1897–98); secretary of state (1898); U.S. Appeals Court (1899–1903); associate justice of U.S. Supreme Court (1903–22).

Charles W. Fairbanks (1852–1918): chairman of 1896 Republican Convention; U.S. senator from Indiana (1897–1905); vice president of the United States (1905–9); Republican nominee for vice president again in 1916.

Marcus A. Hanna (1837–1904): Businessman and political fundraiser; Republican national chairman (1896–97); U.S. senator from Ohio (1897–1904); possible 1904 presidential contender until his death.

John M. Hay (1838–1905): assistant private secretary to Abraham Lincoln, 1861–65; author and historian; assistant secretary of state (1878); U.S. ambassador to Britain (1897–98); secretary of state (1898–1905).

Philander C. Knox (1853–1921): lawyer; attorney general (1901–4); U.S. senator from Pennsylvania (1904–9); secretary of state (1909–13); U.S. senator from Pennsylvania (1917–21).

Robert M. La Follette (1855–1925): U.S. representative (1885–91); key McKinley ally in Wisconsin; governor of Wisconsin (1901–6); U.S. senator (1906–25); third-party Progressive nominee for president, 1924.

Theodore Roosevelt (1858–1919): assistant secretary of the navy (1897–98); colonel, Volunteer Cavalry (Rough Riders, 1898); governor of New York (1899–1900); vice president of the United States (1901); president of the United States (1901–9); winner of Nobel Peace Prize, 1906; third-party Progressive nominee for president, 1912.

Elihu Root (1845–1937): U.S. attorney for Southern District of New York (1883–84); secretary of war (1899–1909); U.S. senator from New York (1909–15); member of The Hague Tribunal (Permanent Court of Arbitration); winner of Nobel Peace Prize, 1912.

William Howard Taft (1857–1930): U.S. solicitor general (1890–91); governor-general of the Philippines (1901–4); secretary of war (1904–8); president of the United States (1909–13); chief justice of the United States (1921–30).

Leonard Wood (1860–1927): army doctor; commander of Rough Riders (1898); military governor of Cuba (1899–1902); U.S. army chief of staff (1910–14); leader of movement for prewar preparedness (1914–17); unsuccessful candidate for GOP presidential nomination, 1920.

Notes

1: WILLIAM MCKINLEY, OHIOAN

1. Turner, *The United States 1830–1850*, p. 280.
2. Ibid., p. 300.
3. *Niles Tribune-Chronicle*, Dec. 12, 1999.
4. Taylor, *The Transportation Revolution*, pp. 35, 85, and 87.
5. Morgan, *McKinley and His America*, p. 63.
6. Ahlstrom, *Religious History of the American People*, p. 447.
7. Armstrong, *Major McKinley*, p. 11.
8. Kane, *Facts About the Presidents*, p. 227.
9. Auchincloss, *Theodore Roosevelt*, p. 9.
10. Armstrong, *Major McKinley*, p. 7.
11. Leech, *In the Days of McKinley*, p. 12.
12. Ibid., pp. 23–24. Of the several major McKinley biographies, Leech's devotes the most attention to his early years. These comments are her only egregious errors.
13. Gould, *The Presidency of William McKinley*, p. 242.
14. Leech, *In the Days of McKinley*, pp. 2–3.
15. Ohio Writers' Project, *The Ohio (State) Guide*, p. 137.
16. *Life of William McKinley and History of McKinley National Birthplace*, p. 6.
17. Hay, *William McKinley: Memorial*, p. 12.
18. Armstrong, *Major McKinley*, p. 5.
19. Ibid., p. 5.
20. Ibid., pp. 10–11.
21. Williams, *Hayes of the Twenty-Third*, p. 57.
22. Armstrong, *Major McKinley*, p. 82.
23. Ibid., pp. 85–86.
24. Ibid., p. 108.
25. Ibid., p. 106.
26. Ibid., pp. 42–43.
27. Leech, *In the Days of McKinley*, p. 19.

28. Ibid., p. 19.
29. Ohio Writers' Project, *The Ohio (State) Guide*, p. 397.

2: SURPRISINGLY MODERN MCKINLEY

1. Early biographers made much of this ancestry in an era when illustrators like N. C. Wyeth painted bold warriors for books like *The Scottish Chiefs*. Olcott has McKinley descending from a Scots highlander, Fionn-Laidh—pronounced I-on-lay—who carried the Royal Standard of Scotland at the battle of Pinkie in 1547. The sons of Fionn-Laidh became MacIanla, and then MacKinley. Six generations later, one went to Ireland as a guide to the army of King William III at the battle of the Boyne. McKinley's own ethnic interest does not seem to have run much beyond Robert Burns and similar music.
2. Armstrong, *Major McKinley*, p. 103.
3. Leech, *In the Days of McKinley*, p. 36.
4. Olcott, *The Life of William McKinley*, vol. I, p. 4.
5. Sellers, *The Market Revolution*, p. 167.
6. Ohio Writers' Project, *The Ohio (State) Guide*, p. 26.
7. Ibid., pp. 54–58.
8. Morgan, *McKinley and His America*, p. 158.
9. Kleppner, *The Cross of Culture*, p. 244.
10. Olcott, *The Life of William McKinley*, pp. 280–81.
11. Kleppner, *The Cross of Culture*, p. 246.
12. Leech, *In the Days of McKinley*, p. 54.
13. Kleppner, *The Cross of Culture*, p. 246.
14. Olcott, *The Life of William McKinley*, pp. 281–82.
15. Linderman, *The Mirror of War*, p. 27.
16. Morgan, *McKinley and His America*, p. 528.
17. Linderman, *The Mirror of War*, p. 184.
18. Armstrong, *Major McKinley*, p. 130.
19. Ibid., p. 42.
20. Ibid., p. 116.
21. Morgan, *McKinley and His America*, p. 478.
22. Ibid., p. 61.
23. Olcott, *The Life of William McKinley*, p. 245; Leech, *In the Days of McKinley*, pp. 21–22.
24. Olcott, *The Life of William McKinley*, p. 245.
25. Morgan, *McKinley and His America*, p. 390.
26. Armstrong, *Major McKinley*, p. 23.
27. Gould, *The Presidency of William McKinley*, pp. 29–30.
28. Leech, *In the Days of McKinley*, pp. 35–36.
29. Ibid., p. 624.
30. Morgan, *McKinley and His America*, p. 159.
31. Leech, *In the Days of McKinley*, p. 53.
32. Morgan, *McKinley and His America*, p. 160.
33. Barnard, *Rutherford B. Hayes and His America*, p. 246.

34. Ibid., p. 446.
35. Ibid.
36. Ibid., p. 513.
37. Ibid., p. 514.
38. Morgan, *McKinley and His America*, p. 146.
39. Ibid.
40. Ibid., pp. 73–78.
41. Ibid., p. 130.
42. Ibid., p. 144.
43. Ohio Writers' Project, *The Ohio (State) Guide*, p. 182.
44. Morgan, *McKinley and His America*, pp. 53–57.
45. Beer, *Hanna, Crane and the Mauve Decade*, pp. 479–80.
46. Beisner, *Twelve Against Empire*, p 9
47. McKinley, *Speeches*, p. 205.
48. Crichton, *1900*, p. 80.
49. Morgan, *McKinley and His America*, p. 76.
50. Shannon, *American Farmers' Movements*, p. 50.
51. Olcott, *The Life of William McKinley*, p. 203.
52. Glad, *McKinley, Bryan and the People*, p. 77.
53. Friedman and Schwartz, *A Monetary History of the United States.*

3: MCKINLEY AND THE REALIGNMENT OF 1896

1. Morgan, *From Hayes to McKinley*, p. 288.
2. Jensen, *The Winning of the Midwest*, p. 19.
3. Olcott, *The Life of William McKinley*, pp. 262–63.
4 In 1881, the GOP controlled the presidency and the House, but the Senate elected in 1880 was tied
5. Olcott, *The Life of William McKinley*, pp. 266–67.
6. Morgan, *McKinley and His America*, p. 165.
7. Ibid., p. 161.
8. Some doubts have existed. The muckraker Ida Tarbell, in her autobiography published in 1939, included an allegation—based on what she claimed to have heard during several years of living in Canton in the 1890s—that McKinley actually knew the size of the loans being taken out with his supporting signature. But none of McKinley's biographers have credited the Tarbell argument.
9. Leech, *In the Days of McKinley*, p. 60.
10. Morgan, *McKinley and His America*, p. 167.
11. Leech, *In the Days of McKinley*, p. 70.
12. Dawes, *A Journal of the McKinley Years*, p. 74.
13. Ibid., p. 67.
14. Schlesinger, *The Coming to Power*, p. 38.
15. Morgan, *From Hayes to McKinley*, p. 492.
16. Leech, *In the Days of McKinley*, p. 75.
17 Ibid., p 67
18. Koenig, *Bryan*, p. 199.

19. Dawes, *A Journal of the McKinley Years*, pp. 88–89.
20. Glad, *McKinley, Bryan and the People*, p. 137.
21. Ibid., p. 198.
22. Not surprisingly, given this relative closeness, some biographies of Bryan devote several pages to charges of vote fraud leveled against the Republicans, especially by Democratic Governor John Altgeld in Illinois. McKinley biographers dismiss these arguments, while conceding that some employers coerced their workers by telling them not to come back to work if Bryan won. McKinley's 1896 margin in Illinois was abnormally swollen and shrank four years later, but even there, actual Election Day fraud does not seem to have been the pivot. The combined effect of lopsided Republican dominance in money, press support, and company pressure on employees, however, is impossible to measure.
23. Jensen, *The Winning of the Midwest*, pp. 155–56.
24. Ibid., pp. 275–79.
25. Kleppner, *The Cross of Culture*, p. 350.
26. Ibid., p. 99.
27. Jensen, *The Winning of the Midwest*, p. 295.
28. Kleppner, *The Cross of Culture*, p. 126.
29. Jensen, *The Winning of the Midwest*, pp. 292–93.
30. Ibid., p. 278.
31. Ahlstrom, *Religious History of the American People*, pp. 878–79.
32. Jensen, *The Winning of the Midwest*, pp. 290–91.

4: MCKINLEY AND AMERICA'S EMERGENCE AS A WORLD POWER

1. Gould, *The Spanish-American War and President McKinley*, p. 9.
2. Ibid., p. 10.
3. Trubowitz, *Defining the National Interest*, p. 57; Thompson, *Empires on the Pacific*, p. 45.
4. The possibility of attack was not absurd. One naval historian has postulated three meaningful Spanish options: 1) to concentrate their fleet in the Canary Islands as a threat to the U.S. East Coast; 2) to seek out and destroy off Brazil the U.S. battleship *Oregon* steaming around Cape Horn to the Caribbean; and 3) to wait until the major Spanish warships were fitted and then raid the Atlantic coast somewhere north of Boston. By late May, "this force could have steamed at an economical speed three thousand miles from the Cape Verdes to Boston or Portland, Maine, lobbed a few shells, and escaped from there to Halifax [Nova Scotia]. Once there, under the international laws of neutrality, they could have demanded enough coal to get them back to Spain." (Musicant, *Empire by Default*, pp. 288–90).
5. Gould, *The Spanish-American War and President McKinley*, p. 18.
6. Morgan, *America's Road to Empire*, p. 25.
7. Ibid., p. 9.
8. Leech, *In the Days of McKinley*, p. 150.

9. *Wall Street Journal*, March 19, 1898.
10. Coletta, *Threshold to American Internationalism*, p. 57.
11. Linderman, *The Mirror of War*, p. 34.
12. Musicant, *Empire by Default*, p. 178.
13. Ibid., p. 145.
14. Morgan, *America's Road to Empire*, pp. 58–59; Gould, *The Spanish-American War and President McKinley*, pp. 45–47.
15. Musicant, *Empire by Default*, pp. 177–78.
16. Gould, *The Spanish-American War and President McKinley*, p. 85.
17. Linderman, *The Mirror of War*, p. 85.
18. Morgan, *America's Road to Empire*, p. 60.
19. Musicant, *Empire by Default*, p. 233.
20. Coletta, *Threshold to American Internationalism*, pp. 94–97.
21. Ibid., p. 100.
22. Linderman, *The Mirror of War*, p. 206.
23. Bradford, *Crucible of Empire*, p. 236.
24. Gould, *The Spanish-American War and President McKinley*, pp. 108–9.
25. As a further brief for McKinley's personal tilt toward expansion, albeit not the Machiavellian interpretation, it is useful to recall his close connection to Hawaii through his brother David (sometime U.S. consul there), his ties to Methodist missions, his longtime links to the probattleship steel industry, his campaign for Asian markets, and his early backstage involvement (by 1899 a tilt toward crossing Panama rather than Nicaragua) in the Isthmian canal debate.
26. Gould, *The Spanish-American War and President McKinley*, p. 105.
27. Allen, *Great Britain and the United States*, p. 550.
28. Ibid., p. 561.
29. Musicant, *Empire by Default*, pp. 556–64.
30. Gould, *The Spanish-American War and President McKinley*, p. 32.
31. Ibid., pp. 128–29.
32. Musicant, *Empire by Default*, p. 667.
33. Gould, *The Spanish-American War and President McKinley*, pp. 12–13.
34. Musicant, *Empire by Default*, p. 600.
35. Gould, *The Spanish-American War and President McKinley*, p. 114.
36. Allen, *Great Britain and the United States*, p. 559.
37. Ibid., p. 560.
38. Ibid.
39. Wilson, *Congressional Government*, 15th ed., preface.
40. Hay, *William McKinley: Memorial*.

5: POLITICAL SUCCESS, DOMESTIC PROGRESS, AND THE MCKINLEY-ROOSEVELT CONTINUUM

1. Wartime generals—TR left the army as a brigadier—who by this point had reached the White House included Washington, Jackson, Harrison, Taylor, Pierce, Grant, Hayes, Garfield, and Harrison.

2. Chambers and Burnham, *The American Party Systems*, p. 162.
3. Kleppner, *The Cross of Culture*, p. 262.
4. Burnham, *Critical Elections and the Mainsprings of American Politics*, p. 53.
5. Kleppner, *The Cross of Culture*, p. 369.
6. Friedman and Schwartz, *A Monetary History of the United States*, pp. 138–39.
7. Ibid., p. 142.
8. Gould, *The Presidency of William McKinley*, pp. 44–47.
9. Ibid., pp. 25–26.
10. Rhodes, *The McKinley and Roosevelt Administrations*, p. 119.
11. Ibid., p. 37.
12. Gould, *The Presidency of William McKinley*, p. 44.
13. Crichton, *1900*, p. 30.
14. Timmons, *Portrait of an American*, p. 100.
15. Gould, *The Presidency of William McKinley*, p. 247.
16. Morgan, *McKinley and His America*, p. 182.
17. Gould, *The Presidency of William McKinley*, p. 249.
18. Ibid., p. 249.
19. Armstrong, *Major McKinley*, p. 132.
20. Sundquist, *Dynamics of the Party System*, p. 141.
21. Harbaugh, *Power and Responsibility*, p. 124, and Crichton, *1900*, p. 108.
22. Leech, *In the Days of McKinley*, p. 142.
23. Harbaugh, *Power and Responsibility*, p. 122.
24. Gould, *The Presidency of William McKinley*, p. 217.
25. Dawes, *A Journal of the McKinley Years*, p. 233.
26. Ibid.
27. Ibid., p. 234.
28. Ibid., p. 235.
29. Harbaugh, *Power and Responsibility*, p. 142.
30. Gould, *The Presidency of William McKinley*, p. 225.
31. Leech, *In the Days of McKinley*, p. 557.
32. Gould, *The Presidency of William McKinley*, p. 249.
33. Ibid., p. 250.
34. Olcott, *The Life of William McKinley*, pp. 299–300. Olcott has not been taken very seriously by later historians. Said Olcott of McKinley and the trust issue: "It weighed on him, and he spoke of the condition plainly and very often, to his nearest friends. His resolution to take up this great question as one of the most important duties of his second Administration is all the more significant in view of President Roosevelt's relentless vigor in attacking the trusts, thus redeeming, in his own way, this part of his promise to 'continue absolutely unbroken the policy of President McKinley.'"
35. Leech, *In the Days of McKinley*, p. 575.
36. Faulkner, *Politics, Reform and Expansion*, p. 266.
37. Gould, *The Presidency of William McKinley*, p. 162.

38. Dawes, *A Journal of the McKinley Years*, p. 192.
39. Leech, *In the Days of McKinley*, p. 106.
40. Gould, *The Presidency of William McKinley*, p. 15.
41. Ibid., p. 164
42. Binkley, *American Political Parties*, p. 326.
43. Jensen, *The Winning of the Midwest*, p. 307.
44. Nor did Truman with FDR's cabinet; Lyndon Johnson, however, would retain most of Kennedy's.
45. Morris, *Who Was Who in American Politics*, p. 312.
46. McKinley and Knox had a long and close relationship. As Stark County prosecutor in 1870, McKinley had sought to close down a saloon selling to local collegians and Knox was the student who provided the key testimony. In 1893, Knox contributed to retire McKinley's debt on the notes the governor had signed for his bankrupt old friend, and in 1896, Knox handled Pittsburgh fund-raising for McKinley's efforts in the all-important Illinois caucuses. (Leech, *In the Days of McKinley*, pp. 13, 59, 75.) In early 1901, McKinley had wanted his outgoing attorney general, John Griggs, to pardon a bank defalcator who was allowed to enlist in the army and became a hero in the Philippines, but despite an army petition, the righteous Griggs said the Department of Justice was not the Department of Mercy. Because of his and McKinley's three-decade friendship, that pardon became the first act of Philander C. Knox as attorney general. (Timmons, *Portrait of an American*, p. 86.)
47. Beer, *Hanna, Crane and the Mauve Decade*, p. 246.
48. Morgan, *McKinley and His America*, p. 504.
49. Croly, *Marcus Alonzo Hanna*, p. 338.
50. Beer, *Hanna, Crane and the Mauve Decade*, p. 215.
51. Gould, *The Spanish-American War and President McKinley*, pp. 60–61.
52. Musicant, *Empire by Default*, p. 183.
53. Coletta, *Threshold to American Internationalism*, p. 113.
54. Ibid., p. 24.
55. Allen, *Great Britain and the United States*, p. 610.
56. Timmons, *Portrait of an American*, p. 87.
57. Ibid., p. 96.

6: MCKINLEY RECONSIDERED

1. Morgan, *America's Road to Empire*, p. xi.
2. Rhodes, *The McKinley and Roosevelt Administrations*, p. 172.
3. Morgan, *From Hayes to McKinley*, p. 486.
4. Coletta, *Threshold to American Internationalism*, p. 15.
5. Gould, *The Presidency of William McKinley*, p. 8.
6. Morgan, *McKinley and His America*, p. 34.
7. Gould, *The Presidency of William McKinley*, p. 8.
8. Morgan, *McKinley and His America*, p. 35.

9. Ibid.
10. Gould, *The Presidency of William McKinley*, p. 9.
11. Linderman, *The Mirror of War*, pp. 22–23.
12. Ibid., p. 183.
13. Two who knew him well and belittled him were also political ene-
    mies whom he defeated—New York machine leader Platt and House
    Speaker Thomas Reed. A onetime close friend, Herman Kohlsaat,
    became hostile after a mutual breach. Secretary of State John Sher-
    man, initially grateful for his departmental appointment in 1897,
    later badmouthed McKinley after mounting senility forced him into
    what became a highly embarrassing retirement in April 1898.
14. Olcott, *The Life of William McKinley*, vol. 2, pp. 374–75.
15. Armstrong, *Major McKinley*, p. xiii.
16. Linderman, *The Mirror of War*, p. 180.
17. Morgan, *From Hayes to McKinley*, p. 485.
18. Montgomery, *Beyond Equality*, p. 372.
19. Ibid., p. 372.
20. Dawes, *A Journal of the McKinley Years*, p. 133.
21. Olcott, *The Life of William McKinley*, vol. 1, p. 343.
22. Gould, *The Presidency of William McKinley*, p. 215.
23. Leech, *In the Days of McKinley*, p. 330.
24. Gould, *The Presidency of William McKinley*, p. 137.
25. Ibid., p. 241.
26. Ibid., p. 7.
27. Ibid., p. 38.
28. Morgan, *McKinley and His America*, p. 64.
29. Linderman, *The Mirror of War*, p. 9.
30. McKinley, *Speeches*, p. 299.
31. Coletta, *Threshold to American Internationalism*, p. 328.
32. Gould, *The Presidency of William McKinley*, p. 159.
33. Ibid., p. 249.
34. Morgan, *America's Road to Empire*, p. 107; Fry, *Dixie Looks Abroad*,
    p. 129.
35. Binkley, *American Political Parties*, p. 329.
36. Ibid., p. 323.
37. Jensen, *The Winning of the Midwest*, p. 308.

Milestones

1843　Born in Niles, Ohio, the son of William and Nancy Allison McKinley.

1859　Graduated from Poland Academy, Poland, Ohio.

1859–60　Attended Allegheny College, Meadville, Pennsylvania.

1861　Enlisted as a private in the Twenty-third Ohio Volunteer Infantry.

1862　Promoted to commissary sergeant in April, commissioned second lieutenant in September after the battle of Antietam.

1863–65　Promoted to first lieutenant in 1863, captain in 1864, and brevet major in 1865.

1865–67　Studied law and admitted to the Ohio Bar.

1869–71　Prosecuting attorney, Stark County, Ohio.

1871　Married to Ida Saxton in Canton, Ohio, two children—Katherine (1872–1875), Ida (died in 1873 aged three months).

1877–91　U.S. representative from Ohio, except for several months in 1884 and 1885 as a result of a contested election.

1889–91　Chairman of House Ways and Means Committee.

1892–96　Governor of Ohio (two terms).

1896　Elected to first term as president of the United States.

1898　United States declares war on Spain (April 25), peace treaty signed (December 10).

1899　Philippines, Puerto Rico, and Guam formally acquired by the United States.

1900　Elected to second term as president of the United States.

1901　Shot by anarchist while attending Pan-American Exposition in Buffalo, New York (September 6), died from wound (September 14).

Selected Bibliography

1: WILLIAM MCKINLEY, OHIOAN

Ahlstrom, Sidney E. *Religious History of the American People*. New Haven: Yale University Press, 1972.

Armstrong, William H. *Major McKinley: William McKinley and the Civil War*. Kent, Ohio: Kent State University Press, 2000.

Auchincloss, Louis. *Theodore Roosevelt*. New York: Henry Holt and Co., 2001.

Gould, Lewis L. *The Presidency of William McKinley*. Lawrence: University Press of Kansas, 1980.

Hay, John. *William McKinley: Memorial*. New York: Crowell, 1902.

Hurt, R. Douglas. *The Ohio Frontier*. Bloomington: Indiana University Press, 1996.

Kane, Joseph N. *Facts About the Presidents*. New York: Ace Books, 1976.

Leech, Margaret. *In the Days of McKinley*. New York: Harper and Brothers, 1959.

Life of William McKinley and History of McKinley National Birthplace. Niles, Ohio.

Morgan, H. Wayne. *William McKinley and His America*. Syracuse: Syracuse University Press, 1962.

Ohio Writers' Project. *The Ohio (State) Guide*. New York: Oxford University Press, 1940.

Olcott, Charles S. *The Life of William McKinley*. 2 vols. Boston: Houghton Mifflin, 1916.

Sellers, Charles. *The Market Revolution*. New York: Oxford University Press, 1992.

Taylor, George R. *The Transportation Revolution, 1815–1860*. New York: Harper Torchbooks, 1968.

Turner, Frederick Jackson. *The United States 1830–1850*. New York: W. W. Norton, 1965.

Williams, T. Harry. *Hayes of the Twenty-Third*. Lincoln: University of Nebraska Press, 1965.

2: SURPRISINGLY MODERN MCKINLEY

Barnard, Harry. *Rutherford B. Hayes and His America*. New York: Bobbs-Merrill, 1954.

Beer, Thomas. *Hanna, Crane and the Mauve Decade*. New York: Knopf, 1941.

Beisner, Robert L. *Twelve Against Empire*. New York: McGraw-Hill, 1971.

Crichton, Judy. *1900*. New York: Henry Holt and Co., 1965.

Friedman, Milton, and Anna Schwartz. *A Monetary History of the United States, 1867–1960*. Princeton: Princeton University Press, 1963.

Glad, Paul W. *McKinley, Bryan and the People*. Chicago: Ivan R. Dee, 1991.

Kleppner, Paul. *The Cross of Culture: A Social Analysis of Midwestern Politics, 1850–1900*. New York: The Free Press, 1970.

Linderman, Gerald F. *The Mirror of War: American Society and the Spanish-American War*. Ann Arbor: The University of Michigan Press, 1974.

McKinley, William. *Speeches and Addresses of William McKinley (1897–1900)*. New York: Doubleday and McClure, 1900.

Shannon, Fred A. *American Farmers' Movements*. Princeton: Van Nostrand, 1957.

3: MCKINLEY AND THE REALIGNMENT OF 1896

Burnham, Walter Dean. *Critical Elections and the Mainsprings of American Politics*. New York: W. W. Norton, 1970.

Chambers, William Nisbet, and Walter Dean Burnham. *The American Party Systems*. New York: Oxford University Press, 1975.

Dawes, Charles G. *A Journal of the McKinley Years*. Chicago: The Lakeside Press, 1950.

Jensen, Richard. *The Winning of the Midwest, 1888–96*. Chicago: The University of Chicago Press, 1971.

Koenig, Louis William. *Bryan: A Political Biography of William Jennings Bryan*. New York: Putnam Publishing Group, 1971.

Morgan, H. Wayne. *From Hayes to McKinley: National Party Politics, 1877–1896*. Syracuse: Syracuse University Press, 1969.

Robinson, Edgar E. *The Presidential Vote, 1896–1932*. Palto Alto: Stanford University Press, 1947.

Schlesinger, Arthur M. *The Coming to Power*. New York: Chelsea House/McGraw-Hill, 1971.

4: MCKINLEY AND AMERICA'S EMERGENCE AS A WORLD POWER

Allen, H. C. *Great Britain and the United States*. New York: St. Martin's Press, 1955.

Bradford, James C., ed. *Crucible of Empire*. Annapolis: Naval Institute Press, 1993.

Brands, H. W. *Bound to Empire: The United States and the Philippines*. New York: Oxford University Press, 1992.

Coletta, Paolo A. *Threshold to American Internationalism: Essays on the Foreign Policy of William McKinley.* New York: Exposition Press, 1970.

Gibson, Arrell Morgan. *The Pacific Basin Frontier.* Albuquerque: The University of New Mexico Press, 1993.

Gould, Lewis L. *The Spanish-American War and President McKinley.* Lawrence: The University Press of Kansas, 1982.

Morgan, H. Wayne. *America's Road to Empire: The War With Spain and Overseas Expansion.* New York: John Wiley, 1965.

Musicant, Ivan. *Empire by Default: The Spanish-American War and the Dawn of the American Century.* New York: Henry Holt and Company, 1998.

Thompson, Robert Smith. *Empires on the Pacific.* New York: Basic Books, 2001.

Trubowitz, Peter. *Defining the National Interest.* Chicago: The University of Chicago Press, 1998.

Wilson, Woodrow. *Congressional Government,* 15th ed. New York, 1900.

5: POLITICAL SUCCESS, DOMESTIC PROGRESS, AND THE MCKINLEY-ROOSEVELT CONTINUUM

Binkley, Wilfred E. *American Political Parties: Their Natural History.* New York: Knopf, 1964.

Croly, Herbert D. *Marcus Alonzo Hanna.* New York: Chelsea House, 1983.

Faulkner, Harold U. *Politics, Reform and Expansion.* New York: Harper and Row, 1963.

Harbaugh, William H. *Power and Responsibility: The Life and Times of Theodore Roosevelt.* New York: Farrar, Straus and Cudahy, 1961.

Morris, Dan and Inez. *Who Was Who in American Politics.* New York: Hawthorne Books, 1974.

Morris, Edmund. *The Rise of Theodore Roosevelt.* New York: The Modern Library, 1971.

Rhodes, James Ford. *The McKinley and Roosevelt Administrations, 1897–1909.* New York: Macmillan, 1922.

Sundquist, James L. *Dynamics of the Party System.* Washington: Brookings Institution, 1973.

Timmons, Bascom. *Portrait of an American: Charles G. Dawes.* New York: Henry Holt and Company, 1963.

6: MCKINLEY RECONSIDERED

Fry, Joseph L. *Dixie Looks Abroad: The South and U.S. Foreign Relations, 1789–1973.* Baton Rouge: Louisiana State University Press, 2002.

Montgomery, David. *Beyond Equality: Labor and the Radical Republicans, 1862–1872.* Urbana: University of Illinois Press, 1981.

Index

ABOUT THE AUTHOR

Kevin Phillips, the author of *Wealth and Democracy, The Cousins' Wars,* and *The Emerging Republican Majority,* is a regular contributor to the *Los Angeles Times* and National Public Radio. He also was an elections commentator for CBS Television News for the 1984–1996 presidential elections.